Getting Started in the Information Technology Field

With or Without a Technical Degree

GALE STAFFORD

DEDICATION

This book is dedicated to information technology professionals everywhere. I dedicate this to IT professionals who innovate, who stabilize systems, who take pride in their work and who keep the customer and the business in mind. Thank you for the work you do, often in solitude and behind the scenes, and often without recognition or immediate reward.

CONTENTS

ACKNOWLEDGMENTS

Thanks to my mom and dad who encouraged my education over the years. Little did you know: buying that Commodore 64 computer way back in the 80s would open up a whole new world for me. Thanks for supporting me to pursue my own interests—you planted the seeds for this book.

Thanks to Allan Tuchman for mentoring and coaching me extensively in 2006-2007. You were a great manager: generous with your time and your advice. Thanks for helping me navigate through a turning point in my career.

INTRODUCTION

I love working in the information technology field!

With this book I will show you why IT is a great field to be in. I'll show you how to get started in this field, and how to develop your career as an information technology professional. If you are already working in this field, I will show you how to move from lower paying positions up into higher paying, more satisfying work in IT.

20 years ago, I broke into information technology with no technical degree. Back then I was just a college student working towards a liberal arts degree in psychology. I had no connections with important people in IT. I didn't know anyone that could give me a free ticket in or promise me a job. And I had no professional experience providing IT services of any sort.

All I had was this: I played with computers and other technology a lot during my teenage years. I had some skills when it came to troubleshooting computer problems. And most importantly, I was eager to keep learning more.

If you have a knack for getting computers, mobile devices, software and other technical things to work, and you are eager to keep learning more, you can break into the IT field with no technical degree. Having a technical degree or working towards one sure doesn't hurt. Technical degrees and certifications will usually lead you into higher paying work. But you don't need a technical degree to break into this field and start making some money.

This book gets you started on the path to become an information technology professional. I break it all down for you. You're going to learn about the job areas of IT. You'll figure out where you'll fit in to this field. You'll see how to find and pursue job opportunities. You'll get help with preparing for interviews to land your first IT job. You'll learn how to build relationships at work. And you'll learn how to plan your progression in IT to move up, get paid more, and get respected as a professional in the field.

WHY INFORMATION TECHNOLOGY IS A GREAT FIELD TO WORK IN

Here are a few reasons.

#1 – It's fun. It's rewarding.

It's rewarding to figure out a technical problem and solve it when others can't. And it's fun. It's fun to help others fix their IT problems. You see them work more efficiently thanks to you. I love this field because we get to work on a variety of interesting problems and we get to play with new technologies.

This field also offers a lot of opportunity. It's a big enough and broad enough field that it welcomes in people with all sorts of different strengths, talents and capacities. That adds to the fun. Diverse workforces are more interesting than homogenized ones.

Since I broke into the field 20 years ago, I've learned that I can solve specific kinds of problems that capture my interest—like problems tied to managing technology changes. I like to lead changes, like getting a new application or process adopted across a large organization or user community. Working with my strengths and natural interests led me down a path to doing "my unique thing" better than anyone else around me. That's a ton of fun.

Specializing means you know how to do important things that people around you simply can't do. Those of us moving ahead in this field IT field have found ways to specialize in something we are passionate about in this field. Through specialization, we develop and then demonstrate mastery in an area. We do things others either can't do or can't learn to do without investing months or years of time and effort. Attaining a sense of mastery in your work is important. That is what specialization allows you to do. Developing your strengths and then mastering specific abilities or competencies needed by today's organizations delivers real value and profits to your employer. That is both rewarding and fun. So come on into this field and you'll figure out what you're great at. Then do that as much as you can, and build on it, and expand into new areas.

#2 – It's a respectable line of work

Geeks are pretty cool now. Unlike 20 years ago when I first started in this field, I believe geeks are now generally respected and liked. Geeky people have helped change the world over the past couple decades. First it was the geeks at Microsoft who created the Windows operating system that ushered in the age of personal computers sitting in about every home in the developed world. Then geeks at Apple brought easy to use personal computers to the market, followed by revolutionary mobile devices: iPods, iPhones, and iPad tablets. Geeks at Google revolutionized search. Facebook brought us social networking and changed forever the ways we all connect and share our lives online. Geeks have built the web, moved society online and brought people – friends and family, coworkers, consumers and retailers – together online.

A 2011 Wall Street Journal article put Facebook's valuation at potentially $250 billion in the next few years. The initial public offering is set to value Facebook at close to $100 billion in May 2012. Many geeks are incredibly wealthy now! The world has changed because of geeks. And computer/IT geeks in particular are held in higher regard now than before.

Like any other field, everyone at the top right now started out down at the bottom. When you start out in IT, you start at the bottom. So you will need to work your way up. As you develop your expertise, and you learn to do valuable things others can't do or won't do, you build a reputation for quality work and results. You get respect.

#3 – You meet all sorts of good people

Just about everyone needs IT to work to get their work done nowadays. This is a great field for people that like technology and like the social or community experience of work, too. A friend of mine provides IT support to the City of Chicago. He gets a kick out of turning on the news radio channel and hearing a story about a big name city politician he helped recently with his computer. One of my coworkers provides IT support to an office where one of our former state governors works part-time. He has fun with his short exchanges with the politician—someone he would have never met or talked with had it not been for his work in this field. Another co-worker spent time working in the Los Angeles area. One day he helped out the actor Adam Sandler with some server problems Adam's company had. I've never provided tech support to famous people. But I've met all sorts of interesting people every place I worked because IT reaches across all corners of an organization. I like the social aspect of this work. Call me an optimist but my experience over the past 20 years has shown me most people at work are good. Most try to be fair, and do the right thing.

In this field, you get to meet all sorts of interesting people from all walks of life because everyone needs IT to work to get their own work done.

#4 – IT offers flexibility not found in other professions

Our profession is fundamentally different from others—such as construction and healthcare—where so much of the work must be performed at a specific location (e.g., construction site, or hospital / clinic). The work we do can often be done remotely, and many of us work outside the office a fair amount. We can diagnose software, operating system problems, server and networking problems remotely with the right access permissions and software in place. We can usually fix the same problems remotely, too. We can also develop software offsite. There's plenty of IT work that can be done easily outside the traditional office.

When I started my Masters degree a few years ago, I had to move my family to Chicago. My manager didn't want to lose me. I was managing a complex email service with 40,000+ accounts. And I had specialized knowledge on how that system ran. I knew its vulnerable points, and how to recover the system when it periodically crashed. So my manager and I decided together that I would work from my new home office in Chicago. For those 12 months that I worked remotely, I came to the office on campus twice. I was more productive than ever.

Two of my coworkers are currently full time telecommuters. Both are productive, and respected as experts in their jobs. Currently I work in a traditional office most of the time, but I work from my home office any time I have a good reason to. I also work from my favorite coffee shop whenever I need to. My manager knows she can trust me to produce results regardless of where I'm working.

Not all IT jobs or companies support people to work remotely. There may be technical reasons, management policies, or other organizational or cultural reasons why remote work is not allowed. But you can get established in the field, and develop credibility as an expert of sorts with specialized knowledge and skills. Then you can pursue those jobs that allow for more remote work if that's what you want. You might have an arrangement like some of my coworkers, who work from the home office one day a week. Or you might work from home or the coffee shop on an as-needed basis like me. Or maybe you end up like a friend of mine who works remotely 100% of the time— from wherever he pleases!

There's another way we have more flexibility in IT than other professions. There's no state licensing for IT professionals. For those of you in the United States, you probably know that attorneys, for example, have to get licensed to practice law in a particular state. If an attorney wants to pick up and move her practice to another state, she may need to spend months preparing to take the bar exam in that state. An attorney could spend a couple thousand on preparatory materials, then take the test and fail to pass. It's something you'll never have to worry about as an IT professional. You can start out in one state, and easily move to another. If you get a technical certification, it is not state-specific. So you never have to re-take a certification if you move.

I entered the IT profession in Illinois. I have worked several years in Colorado and a couple years in California, too. And I've never had a problem transferring my technical skills and knowledge when I moved from state to state.

#5 - IT matters because IT and the core business are interdependent functions

Executives are learning that IT experts must be involved early and often in the planning work that supports broad business objectives. This realization is somewhat new. It wasn't obvious ten years ago. More executives are finding out the hard way that they need to consider information security as central to the success of their business. In other words, the "suits" finally caved in and starting inviting us "geeks" into the executive boardrooms.

Here's an example of executives "learning the hard way". In 2011, Sony was not securing its information technology systems effectively, and groups of hackers infiltrated their systems. Those hackers obtained account information on millions of Sony customers and did a lot of damage. Sony estimated it spent $172 million in 2011 to repair the damage wreaked by those hackers. That damage could have been prevented if executives put the security of their information technology systems at a high priority. But they didn't, and they left the company and its customers' data vulnerable to attacks. LA Times reported that the damage caused by the hackers cost Sony almost as much as the initial damage done to the company by the 2011 Tohoku earthquake and tsunami.

Sony learned. Other companies are learning from mistakes that Sony made. I believe most executives and other leaders see now that it's no longer safe to treat the core business and the IT function as separate concerns or functions. The core business function and the IT function should be seen as intertwined functions because the success of a business relies on effective management of risk. All business is conducted now with the aid of IT. IT systems that are unsecured pose a serious risk to the profitability and success of the organization. IT matters!

ARE YOU RIGHT FOR IT?

If you're reading this book now, you probably already have acquired skills for working with computers and technology effectively. You are probably the type of person that can figure technical things out, troubleshoot problems, and learn new technologies on your own without too much direction and help. You probably started early, tinkering with computers when you were young. I find many IT professionals have these things in common.

Most of us in IT work as a member of one or more teams and work groups in this field. You can expect the same when you work in this field. Solving problems with a team is critical in this field. But in addition to working in a team, you should be the type of person that can work independently to research an issue, a problem or a new technology (i.e., a new application, a new tool) and install it, configure it, and fix it when it's not working.

To restate it, you need to be able to do a fair amount of this research and troubleshooting work on your own. You should be able to function independently whenever that's called for. But you must be willing and able to function well in a team too. This is critical: you need an ability to switch from independent work to either team-based work or loosely partnering with others whenever needed. This is required because of the complexity of the systems we develop and support. No one person has all the knowledge. That's why we collaborate and partner a lot in this field—it easily takes a dozen or more specialists to develop and support a complex, wide-scale IT system.

To give an example, for five years, I managed the campus email service for a population of 40,000+ users. I had a number of documentation specialists and support analysts on staff that I partnered with to support the campus community using our email service. Outside my organization, I also had to draw on the expertise of technical support analysts and staff engineers who worked for an external company that had sold us the message servers. In a few cases, I also had to go to both the director of customer service and a vice president in that external company if we urgently needed more of their resources devoted to solving a severe technical problem. I also had systems administrators in house who kept the Solaris servers running smoothly, which handled webmail, IMAP and POP logins to the message servers. On top of that, I had another in-house engineer who supported the LDAP directory service used to enforce account quotas and make decisions on mail routing. I had a storage engineer who managed the HP storage unit that housed all the mail. All of these different specialists were important to the service. Some days, individual specialists would be absolutely critical to the service when it failed. What I realized early on was this: I had to maintain good working relationships with all these specialists. I knew that, when a crisis arose, a few of us would need to pull together quickly and solve complex problems under trying circumstances.

So, you should be able to learn how to communicate with other peers in your field, and share what you know, and find out what they know. You need to be able to build good working relationships as a member of a team or work group.

There are also cultural factors that come into play. In IT, you will fit in well if you have some common ground with others in the field. If you like science fiction, like using and tinkering with new technologies in your free time, and you like math and science, you will stand a better chance of fitting in. Not all IT people are into these things, but I would say that most of us are.

If you like working with computers, can learn to solve technical problems on your own, and when needed, switch to solving problems collaboratively with members of your work group, you are a good fit for the "getting stuff done" part of IT. And to put the icing on the cake, if you are into science fiction, math and science, and new technology, you score extra points with your peers thanks to your natural fit with IT geek culture—and you'll find it easier to connect with other IT professionals you work with.

WHAT MAKES AN IT PROFESSIONAL SUCCEED

When you talk about what makes a professional successful in just about any line of knowledge work, the research on individual work performance has revealed something. The research shows that it's our general mental ability or ability to learn that determines how well we can perform. Intelligence is the best-known predictor of job performance. The good news is, intelligence is not a fixed thing—you can develop yours over time, with education and work experience. Genetics does play a part, but your intelligence is ultimately shaped and determined by your effort and your desire to learn.

Intelligence is, simply put, the ability to learn. And the key question in IT is, can you make the effort to apply your intelligence towards learning how technical systems work? And can you apply that intelligence of yours to learn how to work effectively with other people? In the field of IT, so much depends on what you know technically and what you can do with that knowledge.

In this field, you will be tested—both informally and formally—on your ability to learn and master how specific technical systems function. Secondarily, you'll be tested in your ability to work with people effectively. Formally, you can expect to have your knowledge and abilities tested when you are interviewed. Informally, you can expect to be tested every day by clients and other coworkers who need the assurance that know your stuff.

Technical ability is critical to both entering the field and gaining the respect of other professionals—especially those who have advanced technical knowledge in a domain. People skills are also very important. Let me elaborate on this and show you why you need to succeed on both the "technical" and "people" sides of this field to establish yourself as a professional.

Technical knowledge, degrees, certificates and other paths to success

With information technology, common sense tells us we can't just walk up to a server in the data center and examine it from the outside to figure out what it's doing. You also can't quickly connect to the device to establish all the logic and instructions that control all the applications and services running on that server. Contrast that to working in manufacturing, construction, or food services. If you worked in those fields, you would be able to walk up to a work location, and hold widgets, handle building materials, or look at and smell foods and spices. You could then infer, to a degree, how they all go together to make the end product or service.

In most IT jobs, you usually can't look at a concrete real-world set of objects and watch how all the parts function together. To reveal a system's functionality, you have to be able to get knowledge from other professionals about how the system works.

Acquiring specialized knowledge on a server, service, application, or anything else requires a set of abilities. You need to be able to read technical documentation including user's guides, administrators' manuals, technical design documents, maps depicting a system's architecture, and collections of knowledge base articles. You also need to come up with and ask good questions of the experts in order to create your own mental model of that technology. Ideally, you should be able to create your own personal, informal documentation—on paper or in digital form—to help you remember how things work.

Completing a technical certification or degree gives you foundational knowledge in a specific technical domain. The domain could be networking, specific operating systems, specific databases, software development practices, or information security, for example. Beyond the foundational knowledge, the technical degree or certification also gives you credibility in the eyes of others. Most seasoned IT professionals would agree that a four-year degree in a field like computer science is valuable for people going up a technical career track in IT, but some of these same professionals will downplay the importance of technical certifications. Their reasoning: having a certificate doesn't mean as much because you might be able to cram for it and pass the test without really grasping the application of the technical knowledge. Although certificates don't prove you're an expert, they do open doors to new jobs. They establish some level of credibility with clients and employers. And they show a certain level of focus and commitment to learn on your part.

Personally I have a four-year degree in psychology, and a Masters degree in industrial and organizational psychology, but no technical degree. And I have just one technical certification: the CompTIA Network+. Studying for that test forced me to learn a lot of fundamental technical things. I'm glad I did it. The knowledge I acquired preparing for the Network+ certification has come in handy many times on the job, especially when I'm setting up or operating wide-scale email services, applications, etc. I generally recommend that people entering this field establish their credibility and credentials by getting one or more technical certificates.

Depending on the job you and type of organization you want to work for, you may also need to land a technical degree to break into that area. For example, if you want to be a software engineer, you might need a four-year bachelors degree in computer science to be taken seriously by big companies or universities that are hiring software developers. The university I work for requires most IT professionals to have a four-year degree to get any full-time IT position with benefits. But smaller companies are more flexible, and may be satisfied just seeing that their new software developers have a two-year associates degree in software development. To take another example, if you want to work in a less technical area such as training or technical support, a specific technical degree is often not required. But knowledge of the technology and how to use it, is definitely required. The more technical the job area, the more likely you will want or need a technical degree to move up into high paying positions.

When you begin your career, much of your success depends on what you know. As you move into mid-career, your professional relationships and your history of professional accomplishments become more important to your career than technical knowledge. But starting out, make sure to focus on developing your knowledge, especially technical knowledge.

Six things that successful IT professionals do on the job

I've watched all sorts of people—young and old—succeed and fail in this field. I've coached people. I've interviewed new entrants to this field. And I've coached committees to evaluate fresh college graduates as well as experienced IT professionals, to decide whether to recommend them for hire. To write this section below, I asked myself, what do the higher performers in information technology have that low performers lack?

1. They continuously learn. People who consistently perform well in this field have developed specific habits of analysis and rational thinking on the job. These habits enable them to receive and make sense of feedback from both systems and people in their work environment in order to learn.

2. They produce results valued by their employers. High performers also consistently apply critical thinking and reasoned analysis to solve problems and produce results desired by their employers. They take some time to understand what outcomes are most important to the clients, the stakeholders on a project, or their manager, or coworkers in need of their support or direction. Point #1 is about development of good habits of analysis and rational thinking that lead you take feedback, make sense of that feedback, and continuously learn. This point is about applying specific best practices in consulting (i.e., establishing clear outcomes for a task or project), and working with focus to produce results that your employer values.

3. They focus on improving efficiency. High performers don't just learn well, and produce the desired results, but they keep improving their efficiency. They record commitments they make in a trusted system so nothing slips through the cracks. They record and track their own progress on tasks. At the end of a project meeting, they ask things like, "what are the next actions?" and "who will do what?" Successful people keep meetings focused so the time is used to make important decisions, get work done collaboratively, or establish next actions on projects.

4. They identify risks and prepare for failures. Successful IT professionals don't just sit back and relax when things are going well. They identify risks and vulnerabilities, and prepare for the possibility of things failing and breaking. They ask things like: Have we tested restoring data from our backups recently? Do we have a disaster recovery plan in place to restore our services quickly if our data center suffers a power outage? Do we have a person who can do what Joe does if Joe were to leave the group suddenly? Good IT professionals demonstrate prudence. They plan for contingencies.

5. They innovate. In this field, it is easy to get sidetracked with firefighting where the urgent things get all the attention. Important but less urgent work can easily be ignored or deferred. Firefighting leads people to lose focus on longer-term goals and fail to tackle the hard work associated with complex projects. We need to regularly step back from the minutiae of day-to-day tactical problem solving so that we can plan and develop projects that introduce new technology and/or work practices. Over time, you should learn how to shift to different levels of focus, from the lowest levels "where the rubber hits the road" to the very broad 50,000-foot perspective used in long term planning. Successful IT professionals can step back from the day-to-day work of firefighting and question the value of problem solving technical issues that seem urgent but really just affect a few people. Successful people and groups shift their focus and adopt the perspective required to plan, develop and deliver things such as: new applications, improved services, new feature enhancements, improvements to the network, improvements to security, and novel ways to support and train users to use all our services and systems. High performers also may innovate in other ways by introducing new work practices such as new team-based approaches to problem solving, or new methods for personal productivity, or new ways to get more work done with fewer meetings.

6. They build relationships with the people that matter. For any job you hold, there will be important people: your coworkers, your manager, your executive team or directors, and your clients. There are even people external to your organization and client base that may become important to you. These could include peers in organizations and companies that have roles and responsibilities similar to yours. High performers build constructive working relationships with people that matter. They show respect for others. They care about other people, and enable others to succeed. When they disagree with others, they do so with tact. They show some sensitivity to individuals and their concerns. They debate and challenge ideas without attacking people. Although the work we do is technical and quite scientific, relationships do matter in this field, especially as you move from early career to mid-career. All people I consider successful in this field demonstrate skill and sensitivity with people. They emphasize both building their technical competency and developing relationships to increase their personal sphere of influence.

Those are the six things successful IT people do at work that lead to good outcomes for the organization and the individual. In the next section I take you further to show you skills that great IT people have that lead them to succeed.

The killer skills to master for success in information technology

Moving into a better job and higher paying positions requires more than "hard work." You need to develop certain skills. Here are the killer skills that I've observed higher performers in this field have chosen to develop, which average IT people usually fall short on.

Killer skill #1: Analytical thinking

Analytical thinking is the skill of mentally separating the whole into parts, so you can reveal the parts and their relations. It is the skill that allows you to sort information. By sorting information correctly, you can quickly learn about complex systems. You do this by creating a coherent mental framework for each system. Analytical thinking skill enabled you to sort all the information you glean about a system into a coherent mental framework to make sense of it all.

Picture a layperson who hardly works with computers. The computer is one big, undifferentiated "thing" to them. They don't know about or think about all the components and applications as distinct things or parts that work together "under the hood". Let's say an application on the computer, such as the browser, is messed up. Or the hard drive is slow. The layperson might think the whole computer has gone bad and needs to be replaced.

Contrast the layperson now with the experts—those of us who work on computers and complex systems all day long, week after week, year after year. The details are what fascinate us. It's our ability to make distinctions between the different components of the computer or system that separates us from laypersons. We can explain how the hardware (i.e., the power system, motherboard, video card, memory card, CPU, storage, etc), the operating system, the applications, the display, and the input devices (e.g., mouse and keyboard) all function together to help people get their work done. It's our ability to explain all the key components that make up a computer or a website or a service online, and how those parts relate and interoperate, that separates us from laypersons. Explaining all of that relies heavily on your analytical thinking—the ability to separate the whole into parts, and detail the relations between the parts.

Analytical thinking is made possible through the use of frameworks or models that help you sort information and data into a structure. For example, when I'm troubleshooting complex technical problems, I sort information into "diagnostic", "possible causes / explanations", and "solutions". I use that framework to keep my head straight, and to communicate clearly with any specialists I have to bring in to help me diagnose or solve the problem.

Whether you are a "fixer" or a "builder" of computers and IT systems and services, problems regular come up and sometimes these complex systems suffer serious failures. We have to respond quickly and with a rational approach. Thus another fundamental ability that comes into play in IT is the ability to troubleshoot and solve problems.

Killer skill #2: Problem solving and troubleshooting

To narrow down a problem to one component of a system, you need to apply analytical thinking to mentally create a coherent model of the system and all its parts. You often have to do this "on the spot" in meetings and informal discussions, to quickly find out what others know, to pinpoint what system component has failed. Analytical thinking allows you to sort all kinds of information into a structure. This structure allows you to problem solve more quickly.

Problem solving is a process of developing and testing ideas to attempt to narrow down a problem to one specific point of failure in the system you're working on. That process – coming up with explanations for a failure, and testing them out, to narrow down the problem to one small component of a system—is the bulk of work in problem solving technical things. It is time intensive, and can take hours or days with very complex systems, and even longer with intermittent problems that are hard to reproduce.

Problem solving is something we do all day long in this field. It's not always a technical problem but it can include problems such as behaviors—things people do in response to the technology. For example, people may have trouble learning a new screen or new set of screens in an interface for an application you support. You have to problem-solve these issues, too, and identify the root cause, and propose an efficient solution. Bottom line: developing your own efficient problem solving skills will set you apart from other professionals.

Killer skill #3: Critical thinking

When problem solving, you try out different ideas to explain what's causing a specific problem to appear, and test your ideas to see if they are valid. In other words, you evaluate your thinking and your ideas. This leads us to another ability: critical thinking. Critical thinking is an absolutely vital skill in many professions including IT. Critical thinking relies on a collection of skills including:

- Skills of observation
- Skills of inference
- Skills of interpretation
- Skills of explanation
- Skills of evaluation

- Skills of analysis

Critical thinking can also be described as "thinking about thinking". That's because critical thinking requires that you evaluate your own judgments—or think about your own thoughts—pertaining to a given issue.

With killer skill #1, we already covered analytical thinking skills and how important those are. Those form a strong foundation for critical thinking— strong analytical thinking skills lead you to more effective critical thinking.

Developing critical thinking takes time and practice. In general, the process of schooling is a process of developing more advanced critical thinking skills. The higher you go in your schooling, the more you develop your critical thinking skills, in general. If you should ever go for a Masters degree or a Doctorate, you will develop some strong critical thinking skills.

But you don't need a PhD to develop your skills in critical thinking. You can develop these skills on the job. If your manager doesn't show an interest in coaching you in this area, ask an experienced coworker if they can help you think through complex problems more clearly. I frequently bring in others to my office when I'm facing a new technical problem or design challenge. I do that to get new perspectives on a problem. It forces me to clarify my ideas, and evaluate them critically when I have another person's ideas to compare to. Most people don't invest the effort and time needed to develop critical thinking skills. Put effort into developing critical thinking skills, and you'll pull ahead of the pack of mediocrity.

Killer skill #4 – Learn technical things

To do well in this field you have to be ready to learn how complex IT systems work, and you have to learn to mentally break a complex information technology system into its component parts on a daily basis. No sane person will expect you to grasp a lot of complex, new technical material correctly, from top to bottom, the first time you're exposed to it.

The magic ingredient to this ability is what I call "focused tinkering". Learning is an iterative process, where you peel away layer after layer of the onion as you go deeper in your knowledge about a complex system. Reading textbooks and study guides peels away some of the layers of that onion. But tinkering takes you deeper and helps you retain what you're learning from the books knowledge.

- "Tinkering" happens when you get curious about a small technical problem, and you play with the technology or fix it until you feel you accomplished something.
- "Focus" happens when you bring some discipline to your learning by adding some structure, setting goals and creating some time each day for both reading and tinkering.

Using an approach of "focused tinkering" will keep you on track and advancing rapidly in your knowledge of new technologies. The faster you can learn, the better off you are. You should see these "killer skills" as foundational to everything else. If you avoid developing your analytical thinking skills, your problem solving skills, and your critical thinking skills, you will cripple your ability to learn how complex systems work and how they fail. And you will set yourself back. You will have trouble talking with other technical people to learn what they know. You will also have trouble conveying what you know if you can't keep it all in good order up in your head. Those thinking skills are critical for moving into higher paying IT work.

In addition to skills in learning new technology, you need some people skills. Let's focus on communication skills – an essential part of the "people skills" area.

Killer skill #5 – Communicate with technical people

Above we covered that you need to be able to analyze a technical problem, narrow it down and solve it, or get another person to solve it. There's more to it. You also need to show your co-workers how you diagnosed, researched, or solved that technical problem. When you bring in another specialist to help you, either to diagnose the issue or implement a solution, you need to have the communication skills to share what you know about the problem in order to bring that specialist up to speed. You also need to communicate with technical people in order to develop good working relationships based on mutual respect.

Killer skill #6 – Communicate with less-technical and non-technical people

Some of the very technical people in IT that I've met do not know how to interact with less technical people such as end users or upper management. With less technical people, you need to keep your conversation more focused on the outcomes they want. You should spend more time listening at first and politely questioning them to determine what they want. You should spend less time getting in to the "nitty gritty" technical details—save those conversations with your fellow geeks.

In any communication, we both give and receive. We listen and we share, so to speak. When sharing technical information with someone, I like to point out that there's a core technical message we're trying to convey, and there's what I call "the wrapper." As mentioned above, many technical professionals go into too much detail when communicating with non-technical people. Instead of simplifying, we make things more complex and confusing for the non-techie people. We do that when we include technical jargon and irrelevant details—doing this only serves to distract the person from what they really need to know, or do.

THE JOB AREAS OF INFORMATION TECHNOLOGY

There are a number of distinct job areas in information technology. These include:

- Software engineering
- Networking
- Tech support
- Training
- Applications & services
- Systems
- Databases
- Information security
- Web and information design

Tech support

Tech support is the easiest job area to start out your IT career in. The requirements for entry-level tech support jobs are not that hard to meet. For most people, I recommend breaking into IT by taking a job in tech support.

Let me show you how I broke into IT through the tech support area. I started out 20 years ago in tech support. And I worked in tech support jobs for several years. I did a lot of desktop and application support for the first few years at my university. I worked hard. Management liked what I was doing. And I got promoted to manage a 24-hour computer lab on campus.

After college I held a couple technical support jobs for software companies in Colorado. I supported customers working in cable advertising and real estate to use Visual Basic applications these two companies had developed. I also taught myself technical writing during this time, using advice from the expert tech writers. I supported our programmers to develop better software by creating or reviewing software specifications. Eventually I moved out of these low-to-moderate level tech support roles and landed a service manager position with more responsibilities tied to it. As an IT service manager, I administered wide-scale applications and services for a large public university. My pay finally started climbing when I left tech support to enter the applications and services job area. Tech support is a good area to start out in. It's a great place to build your skills and learn a variety of applications, technologies and systems. But you usually need to move out of the tech support area to increase your pay and your status in the profession.

Training

Professionals in this job area design and deliver technical instruction and training. They help people use information technology systems and applications more effectively. This is one of the less-technical job areas of IT. It is another job area where you can break into the field without too much experience and without a technical degree. Most people I know who are training professionals do not have a technical degree. Examples of titles that professionals in this job area hold include: Technical Trainer, Consultant, eLearning Professional, and Instructional Design Specialist. This is a fun job area for those that enjoy the social interaction that comes with training and advising others. To do well in this area, you should have a passion for learning and strong presentation skills. You need soft skills including empathy because you need to constantly put yourself in other people's shoes, so you can identify with the feelings or experiences people have when adapting to new software and technology.

Networking

Professionals in this area set up and maintain networks, both wired and wireless. They lay the cable to connect computers and networking devices together. They configure the routers, hubs and switches that keep packets flowing from one computer, device, or server, to another. The network is usually assumed to be working 24-7, all year round. Only when the network is down, do people remember you exist! Networking professionals analyze the performance of their networks, which can get strained as people adopt more "bandwidth heavy" applications such as video conferencing. Monitoring is done through the use of software that collects and processes data from routers and other networking devices. If the network monitoring systems are functional, networking professionals get alerted when a network or subnet has gone down, and they can see which equipment has failed. This is one of the technical job areas of IT.

Databases

Professionals in this area set up and maintain databases. They create data models that represent how your pieces of data relate to each other, and then they set up databases to structure your data according to the data model. They optimize the performance of databases. They restore deleted data. They know how to fix corrupted data, which can be a complex and time-consuming effort. Database modeling and database administration is complex work. Commonly used databases are Oracle, MySQL, MS SQL (Microsoft SQL Server), and PostgreSQL. Database administration jobs pay very well. Database administrators trained and certified to administer Oracle databases, for example, can pull in some of the highest salaries in IT. Even if you don't want to go into this job area, getting some experience with SQL is useful in many IT jobs. I recommend everyone going into IT learn to write SQL queries.

Information security

In this job area, IT professionals focus on securing information systems and data. They specialize in protecting the data stored on systems (i.e., "data at rest") and the data moving between people and systems (i.e., "data in motion"). Common titles in this job area include Information Security Analyst and Security Engineer. Security jobs offer great pay compared to other job areas in IT. It's an up and coming area to consider working in if you want both job stability and excellent pay. Despite the economy and high unemployment rates across the nation, the unemployment rate for information security professionals in 2011-2012 is close to 0%, according to a top information security director at my present workplace.

Applications and services

IT professionals in this area plan, evaluate, and operate the applications and IT services offered by an IT function or company. These jobs usually require you to be on call outside of business hours because you're responsible for operating complex applications and services that periodically fail. You also play a leading role in the evaluation of new or alternative applications and services. At the time of this writing, I'm evaluating mailing list software offerings designed for wide-scale use at the university where I work. Our goal is to see if we might be able to reduce cost, improve reliability, and improve the user experience with this new mailing list software. There are many facets to an evaluation effort, and skills in evaluation of applications and services are always going to be in demand. I have over five years experience in this specific job area, working for a major public research university. Generally, across both the private and public sectors, people in this job area will hold titles like Application Specialist or Service Manager. In private industry but not the public sector, people in this job area hold titles like Product Manager. A Business Analyst may also work in this job area to evaluate business processes and new applications to see how they would meet the business or organizational needs and processes.

Systems

Professionals in this job area design and administer servers and operating systems that host the applications, services and databases. I also include infrastructure like storage and backup systems under this job area. The most common servers are running Linux, UNIX, or Windows for the operating systems. Apple OS X servers are also slowly on the rise. Systems administrators enforce policies for appropriate use of the servers, and keep them secure. One great thing about this job area is the flexibility you have to move around. The skills you develop as a system administrator can very easily be transferred to positions in other organizations or companies who run similar servers. I've seen a number of sys admins move easily from central IT in a large university to work as sys admins for big technology companies like Google and Yahoo.

Web and information design

In this job area, professionals write documentation and design the presentation of complex information to people using information technology systems. Common titles held by individuals in this job area include: Documentation Specialist, Information Design Specialist, Usability Analyst, and Web Master. Usually you need to know—at a minimum—HTML, CSS, and javascript to land a technical position in this job area. Knowing one or more server-side scripting languages like PHP would also be useful in this job area. You should also know how to set up and configure one or more of the common content management systems such as Joomla! or Drupal. Salaries in this job area start out on the low end for entry-level work. But as you advance, this job area pays moderately well. Good web design people are in demand, and are hard to find in my experience. If you develop skills in this area, you can pull in a steady income from your day job, then make a lot of extra money doing freelance web design for local businesses in the evenings and weekends.

Salary: what you can expect to make

Salaries vary depending on supply and demand. They also vary depending on the region you live in. Many IT people have skills that can easily transfer to other jobs in employers nearby. This causes companies to fight to attract or retain certain types of employees with skills that are in demand. The primary way employers fight for talent is to offer better pay. A secondary way to fight for talent is to win by offering better benefits and a workplace culture that is friendly to workers. If you want to increase your pay, try to design your career path around acquiring new technical skills that are in demand, and keep your existing skills polished and up to date.

Here I'm listing average starting salaries I'm seeing in 2012 for some common IT jobs in the United States. For someone taking one of these jobs in a big city where the cost of living is higher, they would expect higher pay than what's indicated below.

IT jobs with higher pay

- Database administrator: 60-70k
- Software engineer. 60-70k
- Security engineer. 60-70k

IT jobs with moderate pay

- Systems administrator (Windows or Linux). 50-60k
- IT service manager / applications specialist. 50-60k
- Network administrator. 50-60k
- IT project manager: 50-60k
- Software developer: 50-60k

IT jobs with lower pay

- Technical trainer: 40-50k
- Information / web designer. 40-50k
- Tech support analyst: 35-45k

HOW TO CHOOSE YOUR SPECIALIZATION IN IT

With any job area or specialization in IT, you need to really find this stuff interesting if you are going to seriously pursue work in it. Don't just dive into it for the money alone. If you enjoy learning about a specific technical area or job area in the same way you enjoy pursuing your hobbies, that's ideal. It shows you have a natural interest. And it will be easy to stay motivated and grow in that area.

My advice is simple: explore things that naturally interest you. See where it takes you. Eventually you should find something you genuinely like learning about which you can turn into a good source of income. Then your next step is to see how to get an entry-level position in that job area. Follow my advice in the "Landing a job" section for direction on landing your first job. For starters you will need to look at job ads for entry-level positions, and see what they require in terms of knowledge, skills and abilities, and degrees or certifications. Ask people who hold those types of positions you want to see how they broke into that area. Then do what's needed to get the certification, degree and/or specialized knowledge that's required. See the section "Charting your career path" for additional guidance on how to design your path onward and upward into this field.

SEVEN WAYS TO INCREASE YOUR INCOME

The data listed in the previous chapter represent starting salaries for common IT jobs. Let's say you've broken into the field with an entry-level job in some area like tech support. Or you landed an entry level programming job or technical internship somewhere. You are learning a lot but want to increase your pay and professional status. Here are some short-term and long-term ways to do that.

ONE: Acquire the skills, degrees or certifications needed in high paying IT jobs

Education is the key to advancement and upward mobility in this day and age. This first strategy is a long-term way to increase your pay. It takes time, effort and money. But the return on your investment will most likely be worth it. Here's a process to follow.

1. Determine what degrees or certifications you need to break into you desired job or career specialization.
2. Research the cost of acquiring those degrees, certifications, etc.
3. Estimate the increase in pay that you can expect in that job for seven years or so, compared to what you would earn over seven years on your current pay.
4. You should feel pretty motivated now. If you don't feel motivated, re-evaluate your plan.

For example, let's say you have to invest $18,000 to get a 2 year associates degree in computer programming. You estimate your seven-year increase in income is $70,000 collectively ($10,000 yearly) above what you would get at your current salary. Well, that is a no brainer in my book. That is not a big loan, and you might be able to pay off such a loan in five years if you are disciplined about it. Seven years after getting your degree, you could be ahead by $45,000 or more even after paying off the loan with interest, in full. This doesn't take into account the lifetime increase to your earning power. It only looks at the increase to your salary for the first seven years. By using this simple exercise, you should be able to sort out whether you have a good justification for investing your time, money and effort in getting skills, or technical certifications or a degree in a specific job area.

TWO: Show loyalty to your employer

Loyalty is not a guarantee you'll see your pay increased, but it is generally rewarded. You should avoid switching jobs frequently. People who demonstrate a degree of loyalty to their employers are typically better compensated than those who are hopping from job to job with some frequency. In general, my advice is to stay at least 2 years in each job when you're starting out. As you get more established in your career, you will probably prefer to stay longer at each job. At the time of this writing, I've been with my current employer for over 7 years. I've advanced a couple times to better positions with this same employer over the years—part of this was indirectly a way to acknowledge my loyalty, plus my hard work. Also, many employers increase salaries yearly for their people who have remained with the company, near the start of the fiscal year. If your employer follows this practice, they should increase your pay at this time if you are performing well. You should also expect an increase if you are handling significantly more responsibilities than when you had your last increase in pay.

THREE: Take a job that requires you to be on call for increased pay

If you are taking a new job or experiencing a change to your current job that requires you to start being on call and available outside of work hours, you should generally expect increased compensation for giving up some of your freedom and flexibility in your personal time. Maybe you are on rotation and you have the pager or departmental cell phone for two weeks every month. Or maybe you are on call all year round. The more flexibility and freedom you give up in your personal time outside of work, the more an organization should be expected to compensate you. But make sure to ask about and negotiate increased pay first before you give up the freedom in exchange for being on call.

FOUR: When you switch jobs, always negotiate for higher pay

For some people, switching jobs is the only time the individual gets a big increase in pay. If you ever receive a salary offer that has no significant increase in pay compared to what you've been making, you would be wise to negotiate for more. At the same time, getting an increase in pay is one of the main reasons to take a new job but not the only reason. Other valid reasons to switch jobs can include: new learning opportunities, better benefits, and less stressful work conditions. I have switched jobs for all of those reasons.

FIVE: Get a salary offer from another employer. See if your current employer can match it

This is a high-risk strategy that can achieve the goal or backfire. Once you have interviewed for another job, and show the job offer to your manager, you can be seen as a flight risk from that point on. Your employer may fight to keep you by trying to match the offer—that is great. Or they could choose not to match the salary. And you are then left in an awkward position if you decide to remain on board with your current employer.

SIX: Do freelance work on the side

If you have skills in web design, database administration, or computer programming, you may have plenty of businesses in your local market that need your help. They just don't know about you yet. It takes time, money and effort to get the word out about your services so, to go this route, you should probably get your own website set up and start reaching out to businesses and other contacts in the community. Be careful managing this freelance work on the side. You don't want people to perceive that it impacts your focus on your day job, where most of your income presumably comes from. If someone does ask you about it, you should be ready to casually give a couple examples where that outside work experience helps you improve and offer more value to your employer in your day job.

SEVEN: Propose something and co-design a new role for yourself in your current job

Pay close attention here. This is complex and multifaceted. It is arguably the most important way of increasing your income. You start off by having a conversation with your manager or someone you know well who is in management. Ask the manager where she sees the organization or the IT services need improvement. Make sure to start this conversation by setting some context and explaining that you want to grow professionally, take on new challenges, and learn as much as you can in your job. Be ready to listen. Write down what is discussed. Also, be ready to talk about some areas that interest you and some skills you've been developing already. Afterwards, sort through the information you gathered from this conversation, and pick out what problems are most exciting to you. And highlight those problems that may demand skills you already have. Do a little research to find what best practices are in use by other organizations that face similar problems.

Now this is the most critical step: put together a reasonable proposal on how the organization might improve in some area. Detail how you could contribute to this improvement. Propose something that could produce a deliverable on in 2-4 weeks. If your proposal is going to take more than a month to deliver on, reduce the size of the project until its small enough to complete and show some visible outcome in a month. If your proposal is rejected, find out why and come up with another proposal based on their feedback.

This sort of approach to career development can allow you to pursue new challenges and put your unique strengths to good use. And that could lead to a new position, and potentially more compensation. It also takes courage and effort but it usually offers you the most rewarding and efficient way to grow professionally.

There is the risk that you put in a lot of effort and you get no substantial reward back from your employer for several months or a year, or more. Giving too much but seeing nothing in return can lead you to feel resentful. You are still learning a lot by stretching yourself into new areas, and you're developing skills and relationships, which is a good thing in and of itself. But in the ideal world, after several months or a year of putting in extra effort, going the extra mile for people, and doing things outside your job description, you have a good chance of getting rewarded with more responsibility. And you should usually see that you are getting to do more of the work you truly enjoy, and you're enjoying higher pay or other benefits from your extra efforts.

There are no guarantees. But generally speaking, you give first and then you receive. So give generously of your knowledge, your expertise, your unique skills and your passion for providing or supporting high quality IT systems and services. If your employer shows no signs of reciprocating and acknowledging your effort, you can always start looking for a job elsewhere where your ambition will be rewarded. And doing so is easier when you have all those new accomplishments added on your resume.

THE INDUSTRIES YOU CAN WORK IN

There a number of industries you can work in. To name a few in the private sector, we have finance, insurance, healthcare, retail, automotive, manufacturing, energy, telecom, and professional services. Outside of the private sector, you have non-profit organizations and you have the public sector: federal government, state and municipal governments, including public institutions of higher education.

There are differences in salary, organizational culture, the pace of work, stability of employment, the resource levels, your stress level, and the benefits you get, depending on which industry or type of institution you end up working for.

My advice is to be flexible and prepare to work in whatever industry or public sector institution has job opportunities that fit with your career interests and values. To clarify what sort of work and the work environment you'd be drawn to, complete the "Career direction exercise" in this book.

Also in thinking about your career, take into account where you live now and where you would prefer to live, and the industries established there. For example, the Washington D.C. area has federal government IT jobs of all types. The San Francisco area and Silicon Valley are loaded with software jobs in private industry. New York City and Chicago probably have the most IT jobs in finance in the United States.

Public sector and non-profits

I have over 10 years of IT work experience in higher education, working for a public university. Most of us working in higher education get paid a little less than people holding similar jobs in private industry. But we get attractive benefits, including plentiful vacation time and tuition waivers on university courses. Everyone where I work starts out with 5 weeks of vacation a year on the first day of employment. In other places, you have to work 15 or 20 years before you get that much vacation. I like having the extra vacation days each year to spend with my wife and kids or work on writing and consulting projects.

Federal government jobs pay a salary that's competitive. Many federal jobs pay higher than what appear on the surface to be the same jobs in private industry. If you look closer, though, the scale and complexity of work being done on IT services for the federal government often blows away the scale and complexity of private industry jobs with similar titles. For example, if you are administering databases for the federal government, you could be managing data on millions of individuals. In a private sector job, a job with the exact same title of "Database administrator" working for a medium sized business might just handle data for 10,000 customers. Government jobs usually come with more stability than private industry jobs, and more generous health insurance and retirement benefits.

Non-profits can offer plenty of opportunity for IT people who want more than just "taking home a paycheck." I worked for a couple years at a small management consulting company in San Francisco that administered non-profit agencies. So I was basically in a non-profit atmosphere the whole time. It was a great experience because we provided the technology support to our staff who ran welfare-to-work programs that helped cover childcare costs for single moms so they could work. Going to work each day was fun because of the great people we attracted to work for that company. I'm still friends with many of the people I worked with then. The pay at non-profits will on average be lower than private industry, but the work climate at non-profits is typically more relaxed and friendly.

Private sector

Private industry tends to move and change at a faster pace. And the jobs are less stable than federal or state/local government jobs. But you can usually count on higher salaries, more opportunities to travel (which can be good or bad), and a pay-for-performance culture. The pay-for-performance culture means that higher performers get financially rewarded much more in private industry compared to those high performers working in higher education and government, where salaries are less varied. Also in private industry there are always new tech companies starting up, especially in areas in and around San Francisco, Silicon Valley, Chicago, Boston, Seattle, New York City, and smaller cities or metro areas like Boulder, Colorado and Raleigh-Durham-Chapel Hill. Most would say it is more exciting to work in private industry than the public sector. Private sector jobs in IT, at the higher levels where salaries are $100,000+, will be very demanding in terms of time. You can expect to work 60+ hours a week at these high paying IT jobs in the private sector. One coworker told me about a friend of his who recently landed a high level IT security job at a tech company in Silicon Valley, California—he is making over $200,000 a year there.

CHARTING YOUR CAREER PATH

Before we start with a plan to get you your first IT job, let's assess where you want to be in a few years with your work in IT. You can do this using the exercise below. This exercise will help you get clear on what work environments and jobs probably suit you best. It'll show you where you'll most likely perform well and stay engaged in your work. When you are interviewing, and you get asked what you want to be doing 2 to 3 years from now, you will have something to say because you've completed this exercise.

Exercise: your personal career direction

When you are marketing yourself to employers, or talking with friends or family about your interests in IT, you should be able to say where you want to go in this field. If you are in a job interview, you must be ready to show enthusiasm for the position and explain why you're excited about the job and the organization that's considering you.

People are more interested in helping you land a job if they see you have thought a decision out. You need to show others that you have a serious interest in this field. They need to see you're worth investing some of their time and effort to open some doors for you.

This assessment below gets you thinking about what you're most passionate about, and why. When someone asks you, "Why do you want this job?" or "Why do you want to work for this company?", instead of looking at them with a blank stare, you'll have something to say!

How to complete this exercise

1. For each item in the "Opportunities" column, rate your excitement level from 1 to 5 in the "Score it" column. (e.g., 1 is not exciting, 2 is somewhat interesting, 3 is interesting, 4 is exciting, 5 is very exciting.)
2. If you scored something at 3, 4, or 5, write down why you are excited in the "What draws you to this" column.
3. Optional, if you scored something at 1 or 2, write down why you're not drawn to it.

Table 1 - Career Direction Exercise

Opportunities	Score it (1 to 5)	What draws you to this, or what repels you
Learning opportunity—people and political skills		
I want to learn how to influence others, support my own peers and my team to be effective.		
I want to develop the skills to supervise and manage a group.		
I want to develop skills for building good relationships with clients.		
I want to learn how to lead a team.		
I want to learn how to resolve conflicts professionally.		
Learning opportunity—business acumen		
I want to see how business decisions and technical decisions can or should influence each other.		
I want to learn the business side of an IT		

Opportunities	Score it (1 to 5)	What draws you to this, or what repels you
function and help with auditing our IT services.		
I want to assess how effective our services are in meeting the needs of our clients.		
I want to learn how to plan an organization's IT budget.		
Learning opportunity—technical knowledge		
I want to become skilled in computer programming.		
I want to become skilled in web design.		
I want to design interfaces to be easy to use across desktop and mobile devices.		
I want to become skilled in information security.		
I want to develop proficiency in Windows/Linux/Mac server administration.		
I want to develop a proficiency in database		

Opportunities	Score it (1 to 5)	What draws you to this, or what repels you
administration.		
I want to develop a proficiency in network administration.		
Social contribution		
I want to work for an organization that is socially responsible and supports the public good.		
I want to help organizations "go green" by using IT to reduce waste and pollution.		
I want to support public education at K-8, high school, or college levels.		
I want to support an organization that addresses social issues.		
I want to support an organization that helps or protects the less privileged in society.		
Variety of work		
I want a job that provides me with a		

Opportunities	Score it (1 to 5)	What draws you to this, or what repels you
variety of work each day.		
I want to work for an organization that will support me to learn and grow in different job areas or departments.		
Innovative and groundbreaking work		
I want to shake up the current state of affairs to bring in new technologies or new work practices based on new technology.		
I want to help my clients or my employer to use the latest innovations in technology and applications or services.		
I want to work for a small technology startup creating a new product or service.		
Other (write your own here)		

LANDING A JOB

When you are looking for your first job, realize that you start at the bottom. Low pay. Low status. Low level of authority. And a low level of responsibility. We all start there. It's humbling!

Your main goal when starting out should be to build your capacity for future success in this field. Focus on just getting in the door and landing that first job. Then you should focus on broadening and deepening your technical knowledge on the job. Focus on building relationships and team skills. Join forces with others to solve problems your clients and employer need solved. Show them you have ambition, energy and passion for the work.

But first you need that job. Here's my advice for landing a job:

1. **Make use of your close friends, your family and close community** of acquaintances as much as you can. Ask around frequently to figure out who is hiring or taking interns in the job area you want to start out in. You will have an easier time getting an interview somewhere if you have an internal person put in a good word for you there with the hiring manager. That holds true when you're starting out. And it holds true throughout your career.

2. **Don't limit yourself.** Don't just turn to the people very close to you for help. Ask politely if your close family and loyal friends could check with their friends, their coworkers, and their acquaintances to see who is hiring or likely to hire entry-level people or interns soon. Most people are glad to help out someone who wants to land a job and get to work. Their next question will usually be: can I see your resume? They want your resume so they can have a conversation about their peers to describe your background, your skills, etc, and make decisions about what sort of position you might fit in. Your resume should make that clear to someone by listing it in the Objectives section.

3. **Help people in small ways whenever you can.** If you're approaching every relationship based on what you can get out of it, you're going about it the wrong way. Connect with people by finding way to help them. Find out what their dreams, goals, hopes and desires are. Ask what motivates them to get up every day and do what they do. Show an interest in people. When you ask for advice or ask people to inquire about job openings, they'll feel more motivated to help you. Show you have energy, passion and commitment to working in the IT field. Show people you will keep at the job hunt until you land your job.

4. **Frequently check job listings and job boards.** Check out websites like craigslist where job postings cost the employer very

little or nothing to post. Or read your local newspaper and its website for internships or entry-level jobs that line up with your interests and skills. Those job advertisements can cost the employer $1,000 or more to post. So you may not find as many entry-level or internship jobs in there as you would on craigslist where it's free or very affordable to post jobs. If you are in college, ask around or check the student jobs board to see what student jobs area available in areas like tech support. That's where I started out. Other people started their IT career in college by programming software as interns for a department at the college. One friend of mine has no technical degree but has for over a decade worked in a full-time technical support job with benefits, as a subcontractor for Unisys.

5. **Register with employment agencies** that place people in technical jobs. It takes a couple hours or more to register with each agency. But it's worth it if they fill a decent number of technical jobs per month through that agency. Basically, registering with an employment agency is a matter of getting your resume, your skills and your technical knowledge recorded in their system. You may need to go through some skills tests so they can establish how skilled you are with certain applications. I landed a few good short-term jobs through temp agencies in Colorado, back when I was getting started in the field. One of those jobs led to a job offer from the company I was temping for. Temp jobs are great because you get to check out the company without making a big commitment upfront. If you decide you like it there, you should show them you are a hard working, ambitious, and results-oriented person by the way you work every day. If you come across a "Temp to hire" job, it means the employer wants to get temporary workers who would consider full time employment with the company after an initial period of time (e.g., 3 months or more) as a temporary worker. Manpower is the biggest temporary employment agency. I have worked a number of jobs through them. Adecco is another big temp agency. There are plenty of smaller employment agencies that you can find through searching for "temporary technical jobs". I also recommend you check out Cyber Coders (www.cybercoders.com) since they have a lot of good IT jobs in entry level positions.

So you can either go through an employment agency or you can directly apply for jobs with employers with no middleman in between. In either circumstance, you need to first build the skills and basic knowledge, and/or a degree or certification required by the job in order to pass the first hurdle and land an interview.

How to build basic technical knowledge and get taken seriously by employers

Let's go over how to build foundational technical knowledge that's needed to land interviews and secure good work in this field. Remember: in the beginning, technical knowledge is your key to advancement in this field.

1. **Use self-study materials.** Here are some examples:
    a. To get foundational knowledge for web design, take a look at "Teach yourself HTML and CSS in 24 hours".
    b. To get foundational knowledge for tech support jobs, consider a Microsoft certification study guide, or a CompTIA A+ certification or a Network+ certification study guide.
    c. To understand basic software development practices, you can read "Python for Software Design: How to Think Like a Computer Scientist" or "Learn to Program with Java."
2. **Tinker.** Try out things you are learning in the study guides. For example, if you are preparing for work in technical support, set up a test computer at home that you can take apart physically or reinstall the operating system on, without causing anyone trouble.
3. **Take a course at a community college** on your topic of interest. Those courses will have plenty of assignments that'll force you to learn through practice and experience. Ask about which associates degree the course would apply towards as credit.
4. **Offer your time and technical skills** on a volunteer basis for a non-profit or your school or church in order to gain experience. You can add this to your resume. Offer to help with their website, email, and general computing needs, if you have basic knowledge and skills already in one of those areas. A combination of knowledge plus some experience applying that knowledge will set you apart from other candidates that only have the "book smarts" type of knowledge.
5. **Take a certification exam when you're ready for it.** It looks great on your resume, especially if you're short on work experience.
6. **Get into college if makes sense for you.** For student jobs in a tech support area, we don't ask too much of you. At my university, for tech support student workers, we're just looking for students who have technical skills along with the basic communication and people skills to help people patiently. So if you are in college, you have an advantage right off the bat: you

can easily break into IT work like I did, through landing a part-time student job in technical support.

How to create a cover letter and resume that gets you into interviews

Your resume is your personal marketing material. It's typically the "must have" document that gets lands you the first interview. Creating a resume is tough. This is where you promote yourself, your skills and experience. This is your personal "sales piece" that shows people you are competent, skilled, and that you have potential. Another critical document is your cover letter, which is required in most IT jobs beyond the entry level. The cover letter may be required by many entry level IT jobs as well.

My advice on creating a great resume and cover letter:

1. **Get a book on writing resumes and cover letters for technical jobs**. Resume writing is something you might research online, but a book on this topic will be more comprehensive and will save you time. Find a book specifically written for IT professionals with loads of examples of professional resumes—specifically for IT jobs. That's more useful than a general resume book written for any kind of job hunter. Technology jobs are unique. Use the book to find a resume format you really like, and mimic that resume format with your own resume. If you aren't confident about selecting a good layout using your own judgment, ask a friend or family member to help you select one. As for cover letters, the same advice applies. Read through the sample cover letters in your book, then a format you like, and mimic it. Always write a custom cover letter for each job if the employer states they require a cover letter.

2. **Use bold, assertive language.** Any good book on resume writing will provide all sorts of examples of assertive and clear language you should be using in your resume. Avoid weak language and statements. Favor bold, action-oriented language that emanates energy and ambition. Don't re-invent the wheel. Actively borrow the language and terminology provided in any good resume-writing and cover letters book.

3. **Represent yourself accurately and boldly.** It's common for people to make themselves seem quite exceptional and "larger than life" in their resumes. As long as you don't go overboard with it, this is an OK practice. Self-promotion is a good thing when you are applying and interviewing for jobs. However, never make false statements in a resume or cover letter. You should not exaggerate your accomplishments, knowledge or skills to a point where you are making a false statement. If you get hired and it's later determined

that you falsified something in your resume, you can be fired for it. My advice is, promote yourself boldly in the cover letter and resume, but when asked for more details (e.g., in an interview), provide accurate information without any exaggeration. It doesn't do you any good to "trick" an employer into offering you a job you're seriously under qualified for.

4. **Describe your accomplishments with a focus on outcomes.** Each resume should include a section where you detail your work history. Let's say you had a tech support job where you also created content for the knowledge base system. Don't just put "Wrote articles for technical knowledge base" as your accomplishment. Make that more exciting and convey the business outcome of your efforts. Write something like "Improved technical support to clients by creating accurate and concise articles for knowledge base system."

5. **Use the "T" format for your cover letter.** You would not believe how many applicants we turn away from good paying IT jobs simply because of bad cover letters. They may actually meet the minimum qualifications for the job but because they failed to present that clearly, they get rejected. Like your resume, your cover letter should detail your accomplishments that relate to the job you're applying for. The "T" cover letter is the only type of cover letter worth sending. Learn this format from any good book on cover letters and resumes. You can also find many good examples online—just search online for "cover letter t format" and go from there. I've been using the "T" format with good results for over ten years. Learning it will pay off for you in a major way.

6. **Organize the content of your resume to emphasize your strengths.** If you have the advantage of a couple years of experience that tie very well to the job requirements, you should definitely emphasize that by placing your work history on the front page. List your work experience in reverse chronological order so your most recent experience is displayed first. On the other hand, if you are short on relevant work experience, but have technical skills or a certificate or degree tied to the job requirements, make sure to emphasize those credentials. You should still list any work experience you may have to show that this isn't your first job ever.

7. **Include a tailored "Objective" and/or a "Summary" section on the first page of your resume.** The Objective section describes your career goals and direction in concise form. The Summary section presents a short 2-3 sentence description of your background as it relates to the job requirements. Tailor these sections to show how this employer's job opportunity matches up with the experience or knowledge you already have. Every resume should have one or both

of these sections. Make sure you show this job opportunity lines up with your career direction. E.g., "Objective – Seeking an entry level web design position where knowledge of HTML, CSS, and javascript is required. Have over one year of experience with website design and the configuration of content management systems." With each new job you apply for, revise this section of your resume to show a strong connection between your objective and/or summary, and the job you're trying to land.

8. **Fix all spelling and grammatical errors and other typos.** Use the spell check and grammar checking functions in your word processor. Have a friend or family member review your resume for errors. Fix it up before you send off your resume. If you don't do it, you appear careless. Attention to detail is an important part of IT work. Typos and spelling mistakes in your resumes will show people you don't tend to the details well. Big mistake!

9. **Submit your resume in Word format unless the employer specifies otherwise.** First let me say that the PDF format has some advantages. It allows you to control exactly how your resume will be displayed to the people reviewing it. And anyone can open a PDF as long as they have Adobe Acrobat Reader or another PDF viewer installed. However, many recruiters in HR prefer Word documents because it's easier to import your resume and cover letter from a Word format into their applicant tracking system. Unless they specify other document format such as PDF or RTF, you should assume they want your resume and cover letter in Word (.doc or .docx) format.

10. **Keep a separate file for each job you apply for.** It can be a digital file or paper-based. When someone contacts you out of the blue one day to schedule you for an interview, you should reference your file on that job before you contact the person and confirm the interview time. Make sure you know exactly which job they are talking about. If you are applying for many jobs at a time, it will get confusing to keep them all straight. That's why you need to stay organized and keep a history of each separate job in its own file folder. In the file, you need to keep (1) the job announcement and job description, (2) your tailored resume sent to that employer, and (3) your cover letter if you included one your application materials. Also it is a good practice to keep a record of how you submitted your application materials (e.g., via email to a specific address, or at an online website for that). If you get called in for the interview, you need to print out and bring those materials you have on file.

11. **Revise or re-write your resume for each new job you apply for.** It's obvious that you need to write a fresh cover letter each time you

apply for a new job. But too many people fail to tailor their resume for the job, which is just as important. They use a generic resume that gets re-used and sent out for a variety of jobs they're applying for. The problem is, using the same generic resume will fail to emphasize important knowledge, accomplishments, etc, in their background that line up with the specific requirements for this job. So the resume is more likely to get set aside for recycling, and these applicants don't even make it past the first hurdle. It can take an hour or more to tailor your resume for each new job. It takes effort. But it is worth it if you really want the job. Just do it!

With your cover letter and resume, show that you have experience and skills that match up exceedingly well with the stated job requirements. Be a good sales person when you craft and fine-tune your application materials. Show this employer how your skills and technical knowledge would transfer to the job they are looking to fill. People reading your resume should be able to picture you working there. They should be able to easily picture you fitting in to the work group, learning quickly, and showing energy and ambition in your work. That is what your resume should convey. And that's why you tailor not just your cover letter, but also your resume for each new job.

Applying for jobs – checklist

Applying for jobs is hard. It gets easier with practice, like anything else. The hardest thing is showing persistence while you walk through the desert and lose your hope. Keep at it. Eventually you'll come out of the desert and take that long awaited drink of water from the oasis.

Think of job hunting as a job in itself. It is good training because it forces you to stay organized, set goals, make connections, and follow through. When you're job hunting, you're in a part-time position in marketing and sales. In this case, the product is You, Inc. The president of this company is you. The marketing director is you, too. The administrative assistant is … you, of course!

As marketing director of You, Inc. you're building awareness of a brand (You) and telling people about the "features" and "benefits" of having You on their team. Your goal is to build some excitement, and get people to take you seriously and see your potential. Handle every relationship with care when you're job hunting. Build an army of fans. You never know who will make that one critical connection that gets you the perfect job.

Miracles of a sort can and do happen during a job hunt. Trust your intuition. If get a hunch you should contact someone out of the blue one day, just do it. It doesn't cost you anything to make a phone call or message them. And it could lead to a job offer. I am forever grateful to my friend Yaniv who trusted his intuition one day, and contacted me out of the blue about a short-term technical writing job with the company he was working for at the time.

That 3 month gig led to a full time position with that same company. It was a fun non-profit management company in San Francisco. I met all sorts of great people that I remain in contact with to this day. One of the people I met was the woman who became my wife!

To help you with the "showing persistence" part of the job hunt, here is a checklist of things to be doing on a daily and weekly basis.

DAILY JOB HUNTING CHECKLIST

- Check job listings at craigslist, newspaper, temporary employment agencies, or other job sources. Note any new job opportunities to pursue.
- Ping a friend or acquaintance in the community that might know about job openings.
- Ping another job hunter (if you know one) to check if he found any recent openings he'd be willing to share about. He might not want the competition if you both want the same type of job, but it's worth a shot asking for any leads he might have.
- Focus on helping others in your network of contacts. Good karma comes back eventually. If you ping someone and you find you might be able to help in some small way, just do it! Maybe they just need advice on a computer problem they're facing. Help them out if you can.
- Keep a log of jobs you apply for.
- Keep a log of people you contact, people you help, and people that help you or offered to help you. Spreadsheets are a convenient way to store notes about contacts, jobs and people. Take note of the last time you contacted each person, and what they communicated in the last contact.
- Treat every contact you make with every person as an opportunity to leave a positive impression, and assert your personal brand. Think, what is the story I want others to tell about me after this contact? That is your personal brand: it's what people think of you and it's the story they tell about you to others.

WEEKLY JOB HUNTING CHECKLIST

- Review your log to see what progress you made over the past week.
- Ping any employer you interviewed with in the past week or two, to check status.
- Look at which people are showing the most interest in helping you. Think of a way to improve your relationships with those people. It could be sending a sincere "thanks" for their thoughtfulness. Invite

one of them to meet for coffee. Or plan a personal call and ask what is the best career advice they could offer you right now.

- Review people in your wider network (friends of friends, friends of family, etc) you could reach out to. Make a note to contact one new person this coming week to find out more about what sort of work they do, who they know in IT, and what they know. Be humble. Ask "do you have any advice for me?" Then follow through on the advice they give. It's a numbers game. Eventually after talking with enough people, you strike gold.

Interviewing checklist: how to turn your anxiety into excitement

Interviewing is stressful. There's no way to take all the stress out of interviewing but you can greatly reduce your stress level by developing good habits. Here's a checklist to build your confidence and turn your anxiety into something constructive: excitement!

DAY BEFORE THE INTERVIEW

- Select your interview attire a day or more before the interview. Appearance matters!
    - o For men, you usually can't go wrong wearing dress pants, formal footwear, button-up shirt and tie, and a jacket.
    - o For women, a blouse with jacket, plus slacks or a knee-length dress, and formal footwear looks professional.
- Clean, iron out wrinkles and remove any lint from your clothing by the evening before your interview.
- Get a haircut and (for guys) trim your facial hair if needed. A well-groomed appearance conveys professionalism.
- Write down your plan and schedule for the day of the interview.

DAY OF THE INTERVIEW

- Exercise in the morning to ward off stress and calm your nerves.
- The meal before your interview should be on the lighter side. Avoid high carbohydrate and fatty foods. Protein, fruits and vegetables are good "brain foods". Your goal is to feel sharp and alert during the interview.
- Moderate your caffeine intake if you drink it at all. It's tempting to load up on caffeinated beverages before the interview. But that can backfire, leaving you jittery and anxious. Just drink what you normally drink each day.

- Review your materials on the job, including the job announcement, your resume and other application materials you submitted.
- Review the name of the person(s) interviewing you, if you have that. If you don't know how to pronounce someone's name, figure that out before the interview.
- Organize all your interview documents in a folder and bring them to the interview:
  o job announcement
  o your resume (i.e., the version of your resume submitted for this job)
  o other application materials (e.g., cover letter? Application form?)
  o interview schedule
  o directions to the interview
  o names of key people including interviewer(s)
  o your notepad
  o your pen
- Use a ritual to get yourself "in the zone" before the interview. An easy way to do this is to listen to music. Rock music works for me—music by Aerosmith, Led Zeppelin, and other legendary rock bands. Use the music that gets you in the zone. Your goal is to head to the interview feeling confident, focused, outgoing, and energized. Read those four words again very carefully and commit them to memory. You can get further into the zone just by repeating those four words in your mind as you prepare for the interview. Your ritual helps you achieve this by taking your mind off of worrying about the interview.

ENTERING THE BUILDING

It's not just about your performance in the interview room. People pay attention to how you treat others. This includes how you treat those who aren't formally interviewing you. It includes people who are in lower status positions and higher ranked people as well.

- Treat everyone you meet in a polite and friendly manner. Ensure that every contact you have with every person in the building is positive and cordial.
- For example, be polite and friendly with the administrative assistant. Be cordial with the person who walks you to the interview. And show respect and kindness to everyone in between.

HANDLING THE INTERVIEW

From the HR perspective, interviews are a way to take pool of many candidates and shrink the pool down to a few finalists. If you made it as far as the interview, you already have some decent credentials. This is your chance to set yourself apart from the pool and show you're a high quality candidate.

- Shake hands with your interviewer(s) when you meet. No "limp fish" grips since those convey too much softness. And no "bone crusher" grips please, unless you want people later telling stories about your grip which left welts and bruises on someone's hand that day. My advice: just match the strength of the other person's grip.
- Do your best to relax throughout the interview, even if it seems impossible to relax.
- Represent yourself accurately and confidently. Speak truthfully about your background.
- Don't freak out if you stumble with a question. You don't have to "ace" every question to land the job. If you fumble or stumble with one question, regain your composure and move on.
- Carry yourself with confidence and dignity, not arrogance.
- Convey your enthusiasm for the job whenever you see the chance. You can convey this with your tone of voice, your body language, your posture, your questions about the job, and the look in your eyes. Be specific about the parts of the job that interest you most.
- Communicate the unique contributions you feel you could bring to the group or organization you'd be working in. You know yourself well presumably. So demonstrate you know enough about yourself to pinpoint specific things you would bring to the position. When you share this, it's also the perfect time to convey your intensity of interest and your enthusiasm for the job.
- Be fairly concise and focused when you respond to questions. Don't ramble on forever.
- Stay alert. Look alert, interested and energized. Keep your posture in check.
- Make a point to emphasize and point out any part of your background, training, education that you believe prepares you well for this job.
- Acknowledge the limits of your knowledge and ability when appropriate. It shows a degree of self-awareness and some humility, which is a good thing to have.
- Ask questions of your own to learn more about the job and the work environment.

- Ask questions to learn about what kind of person fits in well at this organization, in terms of style and personal characteristics. Talk about any ways you see a fit between what they need and the way that you like to work. Be honest. Talk about your strengths and the way you like to work. If you don't have much to say, explain just one or two strengths of yours that would be relevant and then explain you are still discovering all your strengths. Convey specifically how you are ready to learn and grow with this opportunity.
- Jot down notes throughout the interview. Writing stuff down will help you remember important details about the job, important names, technologies they use, etc. Jotting down notes also makes you look good and attentive.
- If they ask you a complex question, quickly jot down notes regarding their question, and your response. If you have three things to say, you can jot down three keywords so you remember to cover all three during your response.

CLOSING THE INTERVIEW

- When it's time to close the interview, your interviewer will make that clear.
- Convey again your excitement for, or interest in the job and why you believe you are uniquely qualified to do this job well.
- Don't expect a job offer on the spot, but there's a chance you may get invited immediately to come in for another interview soon.

AFTER THE INTERVIEW

- Assuming you are interested in the job, and you don't have a second interview already set up, send a thank you note. Send the note by email to the person or people who interviewed you. If more than one person interviewed you, but you only have one email address, ask that one person if they would forward your note to the others that interviewed you. Send this thank you note within 24 hours of the interview. Convey your interest in the job. Give them your contact information and invite them to contact you if they should have any other questions about your background or experience.
- Now wait, which is often the most unnerving part of the job hunt.
- If you don't hear anything back within a week or two, get in touch with your main contact for the job (e.g., HR person, or the hiring manager) to check the status on things. Keep this short. Send an email or make a brief phone call. Just remind them of who you are,

what position you interviewed for, and ask them if a decision has been made regarding the position.

- Continue to apply for other jobs that really interest you. There's no need to stop applying for jobs unless of course you've formally accepted a job offer.

SUCCEEDING AT WORK

Managing your boss

Yes, you read that correctly. You need to manage your relationship with your boss. Or to put it more bluntly, you need to manage your boss. Do not sit idle in this relationship and become a passive recipient of influence, direction, and guidance from your boss. Instead, partner with your boss to jointly identify how you are doing now, and collaborate with your boss to establish how you can keep improving, learning more, and growing in your job.

When you start out in a new job, have a conversation with your manager to ask directly about all of these key things.

1. Ask what tasks or skills you should master. Write down all of those in a document.
2. Ask what specific technical or business areas you should become knowledgeable on. Write that down.
3. Ask what relationships are most critical to your job (besides the one with your manager). And write those down too.
4. As you make progress in those areas (task performance, skills development, and relationships), document it.
5. When you meet with your manager to review how you're doing at your job, you should bring this completed document, which shows all the progress you've been making over the past year.

The secret to managing your boss is to take charge of this relationship. Ask direct questions about what you should be focusing your time on, in terms of work activities, relationships, and new skills or knowledge to acquire. Then deliver that, and document it. Documentation is the key since it creates a lasting record of your efforts made. When it comes time for your annual performance review (assuming you have one), provide these documents to remind your boss of what you've accomplished.

Building good relationships with coworkers and peers across the organization

Those of us drawn to technical work may forget or try to actively deny that political, work climate and the organization's culture (i.e., unwritten norms, values and assumptions that guide behavior) at the office will actually affect us and shape how we work. There's also a world of unwritten social rules that govern how we should communicate and relate at work. And if we don't follow those basic unwritten rules, we may pay a price. The price paid can range from just being perceived as socially awkward or arrogant, to more serious problems like damaged relationships. Here's my advice for building good working relationships with people. You may want to review it before you start a new job or move into a new department. This is my attempt to write down the more important rules for civil conduct in the workplace.

1. Be friendly, respectful and courteous as a general rule.
2. Practice good social etiquette.
3. Be a good citizen at work.
4. Help others without seeking a reward or praise.
5. Don't whine and complain.
6. Don't escalate conflict—be a peacemaker.
7. Be a good listener. Don't interrupt people when they are talking.
8. Try not to dominate conversations even if you know more than anyone in the room about the topic.
9. Show a genuine interest in the people you work with.
10. Read Dale Carnegie's "How to Win Friends and Influence People" and apply the author's advice at work. It's a classic.
11. As you get to know certain people well, let some of the formalities drop away, and build a more personal connection. Ask them to join you for cup of coffee. Or have a drink together after work one day. Building relationships outside of the office with coworkers you like will make your work life more satisfying.
12. Build your own support network. Create your network of trusted coworkers and work buddies. They will be the people you vent with when you need to. They'll be the ones you celebrate with when things are going well. I enjoy going to work every day because I work with great people. I see them as "great" because I've made the effort to develop good working relationships with everyone I can.

How to communicate and work with technical people

Here are a collection of practices and good habits to build in your problem solving work. Collaborative problem solving is really a complex set of skills that's hard to teach. You learn this best through practice. Here are some things to do that will speed up your learning process.

- Before you start to ask another technical person for advice on a system, analyze the system well. Develop a coherent understanding of the system you're jointly going to be working on.
- Before you bring in another technical person to help you on a technical problem, also, quickly create a mental model or model on paper showing the major components of the system (e.g., the website, the application, the computer/device). This is for your own reference so you can keep things straight.
- Refer to your model when you write or talk with the other tech about the system and the specific problem you're trying to solve. If needed,

show directly or indirectly that you know how important components relate to each other.

- If you're troubleshooting an issue, collect any diagnostic information available to you from the application, operating system, or service. Summarize the diagnostic data for the other specialist to review. Make it easy for them to see what you have already discovered by documenting what you did, and what you found.

- Develop an idea to explain the problem. Test you idee/theory out, and record the result of your test. Explain the result to the other tech.

- Adopt a partnership approach. Team up and share the workload as an equal.

- If you are considered to be in a lower status position, offer to do the "dirty work" (i.e., labor intensive stuff, data analysis, log files analysis, etc) as a show of respect for the more experienced or higher-status technician's time. Then come back to them with what you found, and ask if they have any insights into what is going on.

- Always keep this in mind: strong relationships in life including the workplace always come from a foundation of mutual respect and trust. Build the foundation by showing respect and trust in others first; most reasonable people will begin to show you the same respect and trust as they experience working with you over time.

How to build rapport with technical people

If you spend any amount of time with very technical people, you'll soon realize they love to get into the details of the technology. That's their obsession. Their favorite thing is to talk about the fine details of a specific technology that they know very well. They are proud of their knowledge. Deep technical people love to talk about design flaws and shortcomings, and benefits and new features, in operating systems, applications, services, mobile devices, hardware, etc. Let them demonstrate their expertise to you and others!

Here's a collection of advice on how to build rapport with technical people.

- Communicate in a straightforward and direct manner. That's generally how IT professionals prefer to think and act. Don't beat around the bush.

- As you get into a conversation about their area of expertise, get curious and learn as much as you can while you let them show off their expertise a bit. You can use these types of questions to break the ice, start an interesting conversation and learn a lot straight from the experts:

- o ask "what's the most frustrating thing about … " a specific technology they know well.
- o ask what they think one application / server / device / programming language versus a different or competing application / server / device / language. (e.g., "Do you have experience with Python and Perl? How do the two compare? Which one is easier to learn? Which is more fun in your opinion?")
- o ask what they think of the latest major release of application X compared with the previous release. (e.g., "Since I don't know either server well, what's your opinion on Microsoft Exchange 2010 compared with Exchange 2007?")
- Show respect for the mastery of technology and technical systems.
- Gain respect by mastering a technical domain of your own. The most surefire way to look cool and earn props in the IT world is to become highly skilled with an important operating system, application, service, or programming language.
- Develop your analytical thinking skills and critical thinking skills. This will allow you to better interact with technical people in general, gain their respect and acceptance. Most technical people acknowledge the power of rational thought. Courses in logic are included in every good computer science degree. Technical people are human beings and of course not always rational in their behavior, but they do respect logic and reason due to the scientific/technical aspect of our profession.
- Make ongoing efforts to understand their job, their areas of expertise, and their concerns.
- Do all of these things, and they will warm up to you over time.

Remember that when you problem solve with other technical people, you should show them that you make efforts to understand the system you're both working on. Show this by coming up with some sound ideas to try solving the problem yourself. When you are new to an organization, people will always be looking for evidence that you put forth effort to understand the technical things and that you're ready and willing to learn more. Most IT people get frustrated with having to explain the same thing over and over again to newbies. Don't get a reputation for being the person that has to be told things multiple times before he gets it!

Give those more experienced IT people your attention. Make the effort to learn. Do your homework. Don't waste their time. Do these things as a way to show courtesy and respect to those who have spent years developing their knowledge and experience. Eventually your influence will do its work: they will warm up, open up, and share more of what they know to try and help you.

How to communicate with non-technical people

When talking with or writing people who don't have a technical background, many of us also forget to create what I call, "a nice wrapper". The wrapper is your manner of introducing the technical content or the core message, and giving your core message some context. Your wrapper reveals "what it means" to the person receiving your message.

Your wrapper indirectly handles the underlying questions a person at work often has. Here are four questions that, you, as a technical professional, may need to address when communicating technical information with less technical people.

1. Should I care about this?
2. Why should I care about this?
3. Why should I listen to you?
4. Do you respect and understand both your role and mine in this organization?

When engaged in face-to-face or video-based communication, the wrapper includes your body language and tone of voice. Over the phone, it includes your tone of voice, your use of small talk, etc. In written communications, the wrapper consists of the tone in your writing and the subtle choice of vocabulary that conveys a consistent, intentional feeling.

For example, maybe you want to convey a welcoming feeling to invite clients to contact you if they need any support with a particular change that's being rolled out. In this case, you should choose your words carefully to create a warm, friendly tone. Maybe you need a group of people to take action soon to protect them from a virus or other security threat. This would be a case where an assertive and directive tone would be appropriate.

I've developed technical communications being sent out to 20,000+ users. So take a bit of advice here from someone with experience.

Advice for great written communications and presentations at work

- Before you send out or present a communication to less technical people, create an outline to help you plan it. Then carefully create the content of your message.
- Keep your message concise.
- Select the tone of your message depending on what sort of influence (e.g., soft and friendly, or firm and assertive) you need to exert in the different parts of your message. Choosing the appropriate tone is a bit of an art form because it depends on your role in the organization, your status, the status of the IT department, and more.

Choose your tone carefully by modeling other successful communicators in your IT group.

- If your communication is a written one, going out to a number of people at once, or going out to VIPs, you should very carefully choose your tone and your language.
- Team up with someone else if you need help with your written communications. I have people frequently coming to me for advice on their communications at work, and they are mid-career professionals. Don't feel bad about asking a trusted coworker for advice. It's not a big deal to ask a trusted coworker to proofread your communication before you send it out or present it at a meeting. They might feel flattered that you came to them for input.

The conversation is the relationship: advice for fruitful conversations at work

The basis for any relationship is the conversation you have with him or her. If there is no communication between two people, the relationship weakens. If there's communication, but it's counterproductive, antagonistic, passive-aggressive or ridden with unresolved conflicts, the relationship will be damaged. Here are some habits to develop at work to keep your conversations fruitful at work. This is specifically written to help you develop connections with both technical people and non-techs.

1. **When you're talking with another person about something technical, before you start sharing what you know about a given area (i.e., a programing language, an application, etc), ask them if they are familiar with that area.** Then don't tell them things they already know. If you're always telling people things they already know, they will get very annoyed! A more concise way to say this is: when you are sharing information at work, show respect for what people already know.
2. **Watch for non-verbal cues when you are having a conversation with a person.** For example, a glazed look in the eyes can mean they can't understand you for some reason. Or maybe they are not interested. Maybe they are just distracted. Use body language and non-verbal cues to make decisions about how long you should stay with a given topic or a conversation.
3. **To connect with IT people, you should have a grasp of what makes introverts different from extraverts.** Introverts re-charge their energy in a very different way from extraverts. They need downtime or quiet time to re-charge their energy. Extraverts recharge their energy through seeking more stimulation and talking with all sorts of people. Introverts tend to be more private

and emotionally reserved compared to extraverts. Introverts are better at building connections with one person at a time, whereas extraverts can build connections with a group of people at once. That guy who is warm and outgoing, the life of the party, who loves chatting with people all day is a very extraverted person. We have extraverts in IT, and we need them, but they are not in the majority. Introverts are drawn to IT because there's a lot of good work to be done in this profession that is "heads down" technical work, which doesn't involve talking with and influencing people all day long. For introverts, that sort of work is just plain tiring. Build strong rapport with introverts using one-on-one conversation.

4. **Look for the good in people.** Don't focus on people's faults. It takes more effort to look for the good in people, but it will set you apart. Don't turn a blind eye to a person's limitations, and don't be a "Pollyanna." But primarily you should show that you look for and find the good in others. Acknowledge what is good in others. Thank them for their patience, their enthusiasm for helping, their desire to improve, their drive to innovate, their concern for customers and clients, or whatever else you see that is positive.

5. **When you are ending a conversation concerning work, review any commitments made during the conversation.** Or suggest something that you see you should commit to. Don't get a reputation for being the guy/lady that has great conversations that generate all sorts of "cool ideas" that lead to nothing at work. Use conversations as a way to build and maintain your key relationships; but also use those conversations to benefit the organization and your clients—take it from "cool ideas" to real action by clarifying any commitments and next actions that are appropriate, either during the conversation or when wrapping it up.

How to deal with difficult people

It's not too difficult to get along with nice people at work who produce great results and want to help you succeed. A bigger challenge is dealing with the people who do not conduct themselves professionally at work. In this section, I'm going to assume that you bring a certain level of ethics in your work. You follow the rules. You work hard. And you produce results. You don't understand how people can get away with unprofessional or rude conduct at the workplace and still hold a job.

Dealing with people who lack professionalism is one of those on-the-job trainings that begins with your first job, and ends with your last job. It's an ongoing learning process, and if you apply the effort, you can get better at handling difficult people with each new day of experience.

First, let's address how to handle difficult people who may mean well but don't follow certain social rules. As an example, say you have a private office. The nature of your work requires some stretches of uninterrupted time and focus each day. Most people let you work without interruption. But there's a good chance you'll have a person that always barges into your office and interrupts your work without checking first without the simple courtesy of "Is this a good time?"

The way you deal with this often depends to some degree on your status in the organization compared with that person's status. If it's my manager or someone higher up in the organization, I just let them interrupt me without making an issue of it. :) Most managers are spread thin where I work, and are short on time, so they rarely stop by and interrupt me unless it's important.

But if it's a peer of mine that's interrupting me frequently, I am not so accommodating. Peers who interrupt your work frequently probably don't pay attention to the body language you send out, your tone of voice, and other cues that you don't like being constantly interrupted. With people like this, you should have some room to politely negotiate an agreement on when they can interrupt you and when they should just send an email with their request. Or you could ask that they set up a meeting to discuss their issue without distraction. In other words, you should aim to "train" them over time into better habits that allow them to get the information they need from you, and allow you to get your work done without so many interruptions.

Another difficult person would be someone with a very dominant personality. They can dominate conversations in meetings when the issue or topic really calls for more collaborative work and discussion from a wider range of people in the meeting. With these folks, try to redirect their influence. Like an aikido practitioner, you may be able to deflect this person's energy by a skillful maneuvering of your own. As an example, let's say the dominant individual keeps going on and on in a meeting about this new IT service that got rolled out, always bringing the group's focus back to his views and his opinions. To disrupt and redirect this pattern, you can say, "That's interesting. We haven't heard what Jane's experience was of that new application. Jane, how did it go for you?"

Another type of difficult person is the highly reactive individual. Any time they get some corrective feedback from a manager or peer, they get defensive and attack back. Any time the management announces a change or improvement, they react strongly and criticize. Any time circumstances are less than ideal, they whine and complain. There is a professional way to take feedback, and they know it conceptually. But they lack some basic ability to curb their emotional responses and simply listen. A good way to deal with reactive people is to stay centered yourself, and make sure you are calm and centered before you present feedback to them. Also focus your conversations on areas that you both agree on. That can get them to soften up and be more receptive to you.

In general, all of these difficult people may lack the skills that make up empathy. A person with low levels of empathy is unable to make sense of emotional cues from others and unable to imagine what life is like in others' shoes. Empathy comes from set of skills that can be developed. Some have chosen not to develop it.

Dealing with people who lack empathy is a challenge. You might want to see this as a lesson or challenge for you to demonstrate empathy or compassion for someone who is truly under-developed and "immature" in this area. See this as an opportunity to practice asserting your needs in a civil manner without being defensive and without attacking the person. If a person cannot imagine how others feel or experience a situation, sometimes the simple remedy is to provide direct feedback and break everything down for them in clear and straightforward terms. In other words, fill in the gaps that their imagination cannot manage to fill in.

Now that we've covered the people who are pretty reasonable but periodically difficult to handle, let's move on to more extreme and rare cases of unprofessional people: workplace bullies. Chances are you will come across a few people like this in your work. They make life miserable for certain unlucky people who become the targets of their aggression. If you encounter an extreme individual like this, consider my advice below.

How to deal with bullies and other "extremely bad citizens" at the workplace

You have the right to a work environment that is not hostile or offensive. Workplace bullies do not believe in that. Unfortunately, bullies don't carry much guilt about the damage they cause. They enjoy seeing others in pain. They select certain vulnerable individuals as the targets of their aggression and hostility. Then in subtle and not-so-subtle ways, they bring pain on those targets time and time again.

Do not underestimate the affect one bully can have on your health and emotional well-being. If you have a bully who is interfering with your work, do not just hope for the best and wish for the bully or their unjust treatment to go away. Instead, protect yourself and others by taking charge, and taking action.

You should know that the law can be used to protect people from bullies and harassers at the workplace. The key thing is to determine whether the bullying can be considered as "harassment" by the federal government's definition. Federal law prohibits harassment on the basis of age (40 and over), race, national origin, color, sex (including pregnancy), disability, and genetic information. Harassment can take the form of slurs, offensive or derogatory comments, or graffiti. Harassment is illegal when it is so severe that it creates a hostile or offensive work environment. If you have a workplace bully who is taking things to the extreme, you and others may be working in a hostile or offensive work environment because of that individual.

To deal with bullies at the workplace, consider this advice
1. **Seek help from a manager or HR director** to deal with the individual. First you should document specific behaviors and specific actions the individual has taken that reveal their aggressive or vicious nature. The best actions to document are ones where there was more a person witnessing it besides you. If you have any emails from the person that are offensive, make sure you save them and archive them someplace safe where no one can destroy them.
2. **Arrange a meeting with either your manager or someone in HR.** Tell them you have documented the individual's behaviors. Tell them exactly what behaviors you have documented. Tell them you need their help to address the behavior. Share the document at the end of the meeting. Ask for a followup meeting to review what is being done.
3. **If your manager is the bully,** you have a more complicated problem on your hands. You need to work with HR people directly. HR is then responsible for keeping the meeting confidential.
4. **If you cannot get help from your HR people or management,** you may want to go higher in the HR department up to the HR director. The same approach applies. First you document the behaviors. Then you set up the meeting to explain what's going on, and to say you have documented everything to present to them. Present the document at the end of the meeting, and ask for a followup meeting to review what's being done.
5. **If you cannot get management to protect your right to a safe workplace,** you may want to look at the possibility of a transfer to another department to work for a manager that is professional and follows an ethical code.
6. **For serious situations where there is evidence of discrimination,** you may want to consider filing a charge of discrimination with the U.S. Equal Employment Opportunity Commission. If you have something to report, and you have decided the filing a charge is what you would like to do, you should report it as soon as possible. That is because the EEOC requires the charge to be filed within 180 calendar days from the day the discrimination took place.

Some employers have policies that punish workplace bullies. For example, if it's made known that a person leaves the organization because another employee made their life at work unbearable, the bully loses their job too. It's as simple as that.

How to deal with slights

If you feel slighted by someone, it's because you perceive they have not treated you with proper respect. You probably believe they treated you unfairly in some way. And you are probably right. But, as my favorite business consultant Alan Weiss says, you should either find a civil way to address it with the person or just forget about it and put it behind you. If you keep running a story in your head about how terrible that person is, and you keep running a negative story line every time you see or think about them, the slight—whether real or completely imagined—will stay with you forever.

How to build good relationships with clients through great communication

When I was younger, I thought the technical stuff in this field mattered most. And I figured I could just ignore the political/people side of work. I would join in with others when they said office politics were so silly. But as I gained experience and completed some challenging wide-scale IT projects that touched thousands of people, I came to see things in a new light. I still believe the technology must reliably work and fit people's needs. And the technical content in our communications with clients and coworkers has to be accurate and coherent. But the political side of IT work is critically important especially in large organizations. The wrapper we create around our communications—including proper handling of the political aspect of technology changes—can make all the difference in the world. This is especially true if you are responsible for communicating a lot with end users, managers, and directors about new and changing services and technology.

Let me give an example. Recently I worked on a major IT project to retire an email service for 30,000 college students. We had a communications specialist on the project team to help us plan our communications to the students and other stakeholders on campus. She also wrote many of our communications. What was interesting was, the first message that went to the 30,000 students was pretty friendly and positive. We told them about this new email service we had arranged for them to use. It was our own private Google Apps for Education domain, which included the email, calendaring, chat, docs, and other popular applications from Google—in a domain we administered privately. Our message to the students emphasized the benefits of this new service and gently invited them to go sign up for it. The response was dismal. Very few students signed up for the new service. And we had a deadline to meet!

I decided we needed to change the tone of the message to a more assertive one, emphasizing what they were about to lose instead of what they were going to gain. So the next message that went out emphasized they were going to lose their account on the current email system by this fast-approaching date. It emphasized taking quick action to avoid losing their email. The response was terrific. We emphasized the negative consequences (i.e., lost email) that we knew they wanted to avoid. The project was a great success because we changed both our core message and the tone of our communication from warm and friendly to assertive, bold and directive.

I'm sure you've noticed a tactic used by major political campaigns that aim to influence millions of people: the use of negative messages. Negative messages are more motivating than positive ones. The same thing goes for communications in IT. Often when the soft approach fails, we have to use a more assertive approach to get people off of their old systems and computers because change is difficult. Many people like using what's familiar to them even if it's old and outdated. We sometimes need to be very direct, and establish deadlines, and state clearly they are going to lose (e.g., valuable data, valuable email, etc) if they fail to take action.

But as a general rule, when you communicate with clients, you should get in a habit of adding a friendly wrapper around it. If it's a new client, be especially formal and friendly on the first meeting. Being more formal means you show extra respect, try to make them feel a little dignified, and generally follow social rules and social etiquette with greater consistency than usual. As you get to know your clients, you will learn how formal they prefer to be when interacting with you, and you can adjust (down or up) to the level of formality they show you. It's always safer to show more formality when dealing with clients than with your peers and coworkers.

How to help clients who are seriously frustrated with a technical problem

When a client of yours is struggling with a technical problem, this can go one of two ways for you. Either the person is relieved and comforted by how helpful or knowledgeable you are. Or they get even more frustrated by the way you handle the situation. Here are some pointers based on what I've learned while supporting customers over the past couple decades:

1. **Show warmth and patience** throughout the customer support session. Be like a doctor with good bedside manners. Choose your tone of voice, your body language, and your vocabulary to convey respect and kindness.
2. **Use the phrase "I'm sorry this is so frustrating"** to show empathy and sensitivity to their situation.

3. **Your first goal: show to the client that, without a doubt, you want to help them.** Making it clear and obvious that you do want to help. "Let me see what I can do to help you out today. If I can't solve your problem, I will get someone else who can."

4. **Your second goal: gather diagnostics.** Ask questions tactfully to figure out what happened. Do this before you dive into the problem and start changing their computer, device, website configuration or other settings. Explain that the diagnostic questions help you narrow down the problem.

5. **When you have some ideas on what could be causing it,** ask their permission to try out something that may fix it. Asking permission displays good etiquette. It also gives that person a feeling of control again.

6. **When you have it figured out, or have decided you cannot figure it out,** explain to your client what was going on in plain English using terms, using vocabulary they understand.

7. **If you cannot figure it out, explain to your client what's going on.** It could be that you've never encountered an issue quite like this one. Just be honest.

8. **Remain humble and helpful.** Avoid arrogance or aloofness in any form. When we have specialized knowledge and some well-developed analytic and critical thinking skills, we may get a little "too smart for our own good" in some cases. If you lack warmth and respect, your frustrated client will get even more frustrated!

Your specialized knowledge of the system and your critical thinking skill combined are what enable you to understand what's going on "under the hood." Don't let it go to your head. Your client's perceptions of you are important. Client satisfaction or peer evaluations of you could be an important factor your supervisor uses to determine how well you are performing overall at work. You advance in your career more quickly when you have a network of supporters and allies across your workplace. Don't become overly "task oriented" in your work. Remember that it's both high "task performance" coupled with high quality work relationships that leads to long-term career success.

Develop good communication habits. Select the right language, the right tone of voice, and the right manner of asking questions to impress clients with your professionalism and tact. You will go farther as a leader than IT professionals who lack these habits.

How to excel on a team

Working in a team effectively requires specific skills. No one ever broke this down for me when I started out in this field. I had to learn it on my own over time. I also read a lot over the years on the psychology of teams, conflict resolution, and performance. Recently I helped set the performance standards for information technology at the public university I work for. This will determine how hundreds of technology professionals are assessed for years to come. I believe many organizations have a similar set of standards for team performance. Here are some of the standards I helped set for the organization, plus some of my own beliefs in the area of team performance:

- Be ready and willing to take on different roles periodically as a member of a team. For example, a team member is out sick for a week, and someone needs to cover his responsibilities. Be ready to step up to the plate and take on some extra work, doing work you don't normally do. A key quality we want to see here is flexibility and a desire to help others on the team even when it's hard.

- Apologize when you screw up. We make mistakes. That is part of the process of learning and growing as a professional. How you handle your own professional mistakes and errors in judgment is up to you. Admitting a mistake shows humility. Don't be so rigid or arrogant that you cannot say "sorry" when you made a mistake or had a major screwup at work. Also if it was a major screwup, create a plan to prevent that from occurring again, and be ready to tell others how you will prevent it.

- Plan and coordinate work with your team. This requires good communication and goal-setting skills. You have to, as a team, look at what work must be done, and split up the work fairly and according to areas of expertise. This also requires some negotiation skills, and it can be difficult to sort through conflicts of "who does what" when some of the work is more desirable than other

- Negotiate and sort through conflict respectfully. When negotiating "who does what", be ready to assert yourself while respecting others views. Also be ready to yield on some decisions, and assert your needs on other decisions that are more important to you. This is challenging. Working through conflicts about "who does what" is a critically important skill in teams.

- Give frequent positive feedback to team members. The easiest type of feedback to give is the "pat on the back" when someone has done well. So, give that sort of feedback as often as you see fit. The more, the better. This is a kind gesture and it helps people recognize their strengths. In doing this, you create a team climate that lifts people up.

- Give developmental feedback carefully if someone needs it. There are times when things didn't work out too well for a team member. And that person on your team may need to develop and improve in an area of their job. They may need that feedback from you specifically to improve in that area. For example, maybe their communication style with a difficult customer is only making things worse, and escalating the conflicts that come up with when that very demanding customer doesn't get what they want. Your team member needs the feedback, but how do you give it? This sort of feedback has to be given carefully. Usually you should give this sort of feedback to your team mate in a private one-on-one conversation. Many people cannot take "developmental feedback" like this very well, and they may get defensive when you tell them something could have been done differently to get a better outcome for everyone involved. So you have to think about whether you care enough to bring an issue up with them. You also have to think about the strength of your relationship with that person, too, and your status in the organization or team compared to their status. There are usually unspoken and unwritten rules in the team or organization that say newer people cannot give certain types of feedback to the more experienced professionals. So, respect the code of conduct. Ask a peer for advice or ask your manager or mentor for advice if you want to figure out how to give these more difficult forms of feedback to another person who seems to need it.

- As a newcomer to a team, always respect the code of conduct. Take some time when you join a new team to understand the code of conduct in the team and the organization. Respect the rules as a newcomer, and don't try to rock the boat too much. After you've shown respect for "the code" you can slowly start to suggest new ways of doing things as you see fit. Or just model the new way of doing things without talking about it or trying to sell anyone on it. But first, take time to understand and show respect for the way things are done, because there are reasons for the code of conduct, and people usually want you to acknowledge that.

Many of these team skills are only learned through on-the-job experiences. One day you'll just find yourself suddenly in a difficult situation where there's a conflict with a team member, and you realize you need to work through that. This is your learning opportunity so handle these situations with care and ask for help when you need it.

Don't underestimate the challenges and the rewards of working in teams. Much of your career growth will be enhanced if you can support others to succeed as a team member on a short-term project or a long-term "functional team". Much of your work in IT will be "solo" as well, but team performance is a critical element of working in information technology in most organizations. And due to the complexity of our systems, where many specialists are required to develop or maintain an application, network, or service, team performance will remain important for years to come.

CHEAT SHEETS – FOUNDATIONAL TECHNICAL KNOWLEDGE

When you are just getting into the field, and landing one of your first jobs in IT, people won't expect too much of you. But the more you know at the time of your interview and on the first day of your job, the more you set yourself apart from other new entrants into the field. Knowing more of the basic "nuts and bolts" stuff of IT generally shows you have ambition and focus. It shows you have a genuine interest in and commitment to the field. I created this section as a cheat sheet. It's a summary of basic knowledge that hiring managers and experienced IT / human resource professionals like me want all new people coming into the field to know. Or if they don't know it, most of us want you to learn this stuff within, say, your first 3-6 months of entering the field.

The client-server model

The input of data, the processing and the validation of data, and the output of data are split up between the two parts of this model. One part of this model or system is the client (e.g., a web browser). Another part is the server (e.g., a web application hosted on a server). Usually, applications are designed to hold almost all the logic and "smarts" for processing data in the application, which is running on a server. So we have the "heavy lifting" being done by the server. However there are advantages to including some of the data processing, some of the "smarts" or the logic down at the client level.

Let me give an example. You can include some data validation code in your web app that is handled by the web browser (i.e., the client) instead of up on the server. This code could, for example, verify whether a password string meets a few minimum requirements. Having this code executed by the web browser allows the user to receive immediate on-screen feedback such as "Your password isn't long enough. It must be at least eight characters.", before the user submits the new password up to the application on the server. This is an example of including a bit of useful code and logic in the client. But generally speaking, we usually architect our systems to include the bulk of the logic and processing power on the server, and we keep our clients pretty "thin" and store relatively little logic in them.

On-site servers versus cloud-based servers/services

Hosting your IT services fully in-house or "on premise" requires a lot of work and is costly. That's why many businesses are outsourcing certain IT services to the cloud. Email is a good example. I recently handled a major project where we outsourced email, calendaring, and office applications for

30,000+ undergraduate students to Google. The advantage of hosting services "on premise" is the control you have. There are ways to secure data stored in the cloud, but generally if the organization wants to be sure data is kept safe and secure, they will host the service and database on premise—not up in the cloud. There is huge growth coming in cloud-based services because it is a lower cost, efficient way to get software. When someone else takes care of the maintenance and upgrades, you don't have to staff internal people to do all of the software maintenance work "locally" anymore. Software-as-a-service (SaaS) is a relatively new software delivery model, with $10 billion in sales for 2010, with projected sales in 2015 reaching over $20 billion, according to the Gartner Group analysts.

Project management models

If you know and adhere to some basics when you work on a major project, your life will improve at work. Project management relies on an established body of knowledge, skills and practices that guide how any complex project should be handled.

The three phases of a project are: (1) the "requirements specification" in which you detail what the system under development must do, (2) the "system development" in which you create and integrate the system specified in the previous step, (3) and "systems and requirements validation" in which you validate that the system developed meets the original specification.

This model is expressed in something known as the "V model". When a project begins, the project team starts their work at the "left arm" of the V. They complete the requirements analysis, the system design and architecture. Then they move to the bottom tip of the V where the team handles coding and implementation of the requirements and architecture. Lastly, the team moves to activities in the "right arm" of the V. They handle system validation (e.g., unit testing, integration testing), and requirements validation (acceptance testing). Do an online search on the "V model project management" to see examples of this. Project management skills and know-how will help you in your career.

Networking

There's a lot going on under the hood in your home or office network that you don't need to know about. But you should study up on this area to at least learn about network packets. You should learn about routers, switches, and hubs. They are network devices that send packets to where they need to get in a network. You should also learn about the OSI model. This is a model that includes 7 layers: the Physical, Data, Network, Transport, Session, Presentation, and Application layers.

Network protocols you should know

Protocol	What you should know about it
IMAP (Internet Message Access Protocol)	An IMAP server listens on port 143; for secure IMAP, a server listens on port 993;
POP (Post Office Protocol)	Like IMAP, it's a commonly used protocol for mail retrieval; a POP server typically listens on well-known port 110 for POP requests for mail; a secure POP server typically listens on well-known port 995;
HTTP (Hypertext transfer protocol)	Port 80; most web traffic is sent using this protocol;
HTTPS	Port 443; encrypted web traffic is sent using this combination of HTTP with SSL/TLS protocol
SSL/TLS	Secure Sockets Layer and Transport Layer Security are both cryptographic protocols. SSL is the predecessor to TLS. They provide a way for servers and clients to securely communicate over the Internet.
SSH (Secure shell)	The well-known port 22 is commonly used for SSH; used for secure logins to a remote computer and securely issuing commands; allows for copying of files using secure ftp (SFTP) commands and secure copy (SCP) commands.
telnet	The well-known port 23 is commonly used for telnet; It's a protocol for interactive bi-directional text-oriented communications between servers or between client and server. Because telnet is not secure, its usage has been dropping rapidly for years, while SSH usage increases. All transmissions sent over telnet are in clear text.

FTP (File transfer protocol)	Well-known port 20 typically used for data transfer. Port 21 for commands; It's a way to transfer files where security is not important. Like telnet, usage of FTP is dropping while secure FTP usage increases. FTP transmissions are in clear text.

Backups and restores

Every IT professional should have a grasp of basic technologies available for backing up data and restoring it. For example, there are consumer-oriented data backup services, which involve installation of a client on the person's desktop or laptop computer, which backs up data to a server each night. Then there are backup services for servers, which take massive amounts of data from servers and back them up to tape each night, for example. You should know for your own sake where your data at work is getting backed up, and how you can restore it if needed. In my work, most of the data I am responsible for protecting is stored on servers in our data center. I know if I delete an important file on the server, I can go to my system administrator for that server to get the file restored. I store many of my work documents on my laptop in a folder that syncs up to the Box.net account made available by my employer. So I have a copy stored securely up in the cloud if I ever lose my local copy.

Software development models – waterfall versus agile

Development of software begins with a functional requirements specification. Using this requirements specification, a technical design is created. Then the actual software is coded. When coding is done, unit testing is conducted, and low-level bugs are fixed. Then user acceptance testing is conducted, and the bugs found at that level of testing are fixed. Then you typically have a pilot group of users try out the software so additional bugs can be worked out before it gets rolled out to all users. Software development is hard work and more complex and time-intensive than people think.

There are two approaches to software development. One is the traditional approach that requires a lot of upfront planning and technical design before any code is written. Then the code is written over months, tested, bugs are fixed, and then it's released. This is called the "waterfall model".

The newer approach emphasizes less upfront planning and technical design, and shorter release cycles. In this approach, you do not try to plan and design everything upfront. You plan something small, code it, test it, and release it. Then you plan another small improvement, and code, then release again in just a week or two. This is the "agile model" for software development.

The trend is moving in favor of agile software development models with short release cycles, because this approach responds better to changes in requirements. People using the waterfall model for software development usually make too many assumptions about requirements not changing, which don't hold up to reality. For example, using the waterfall model, you spend two months upfront creating this great plan and design document, then you get coding for a couple months. Four months into the project, a few new requirements show up that make your initial requirements doc and design specification completely invalid. So you have to stop development, go back to the requirements and design docs again, and revise the plan in a major way. You end up throwing out and revising a lot of plans or code that you spent weeks writing. Agile development can avoid this problem and can usually save companies money and time over the waterfall model. Agile models for development are appropriate for many types of software development projects but not all of them. So if an organization uses the waterfall model, don't assume it's the wrong model for them.

Secure computing best practices

I manage the onboarding program for new hires at the university where I work. There are over 250 IT professionals in my organization, and 20-30 new hires coming on board each year. One thing we cover with new hires is how to get your work done safely and securely. This is very important. You should know about and follow some standard practices to follow in order to protect your data, your client's data, your employer's data, and equipment. You must understand that protecting your client's data and employer's data is incredibly important.

1. Use strong passwords with a combination of uppercase and lowercase letters, numbers and punctuation marks.
2. Store your passwords in an encrypted format using an application designed for that. I use Password Vault at my job. Your employer may provide a password storage application for you to store all your work passwords.
3. Keep an encrypted copy of your password file in more than one place. E.g., store one encrypted copy on your computer or laptop's hard drive, then keep a second encrypted copy on a USB stick. Create a reminder on your calendar to sync up the two copies weekly, monthly, or as often as required.
4. Protect your physical equipment from theft. Guard your laptop when you're working at a library or coffee shop. If you spend a lot of time at coffee shops like me, you might even want to buy a laptop security cable to secure your laptop to the table.
5. Password-protect your laptop, desktop computer and other mobile devices.

6. Avoid storing sensitive data on your laptop. This can include customer data such as credit card numbers, social security numbers, medical records, and tax information. Laptops are easy to steal. If you must work with sensitive data on your laptop, see if you can find a way to download the data to your laptop for the day, then delete it before the end of your workday. Generally, try to keep all sensitive data safely tucked away on a secure server and off of your laptop, mobile device or other computer.

7. If you must store sensitive data on your laptop, use software to encrypt all the data on your hard drive. TrueCrypt is a free, open source on-the-fly encryption solution that my friends in information security would recommend.

8. Report theft immediately. If your computer, laptop, smartphone or other mobile device for work is stolen, report it to your information security department or IT director at work. If you have the capability to do a "remote wipe" of your mobile device to wipe it clean of all your data, they can help you do that immediately. They can tell you how to go about notifying the police. If you cannot remotely wipe your mobile device clean, you should immediately change your passwords on your work email account. Change passwords for all the cloud services you've configured your computer or mobile device to access. The faster you change your passwords, the better off you are.

9. Transmit passwords over secure channels, such as a secure chat session.

10. Create separate admin accounts for each user if you are ever the top administrator for a service, application or operating system with multiple admin users. Shared admin accounts are a poor solution because you can't audit access or easily grant/revoke access as individuals join or leave your workgroup.

11. Never give your work passwords out to anyone. If you get a suspicious email asking you to visit a website and enter your password, delete it. If a spouse, significant other, or family member asks for your work password for some reason, just tell them it's against company policy and you want to respect the policy and stay out of trouble.

CLOSING WORDS

Now that you've gotten this far in the book, I hope you are excited about entering the field of IT, and advancing your career. Here are some closing words of advice.

I've stressed that the ability to learn is fundamental to breaking into IT and pulling ahead. More specifically, you need to make consistently strong efforts at learning new material related to computers, applications, and information technology in general. You should also make the effort to learn better ways of communicating with people and influencing or guiding people including co-workers, managers and clients you provide services to. This means you allocate part of your income for training and certifications, as needed, to advance yourself. It's not a bad idea to allocate 2-3% of your income to training and education if you're sure those new skills, knowledge, etc, will take you forward. So, you must be ready and willing to invest both time, effort, and money into building your capacity for success.

So, keep learning. Don't get lazy. Make the effort. Pursue your interests and your curiosities. Explore new technologies, new ways of leading people, new ways of communicating with clients and coworkers. If you stay disciplined and keep your focus on learning new things every day at your job, you'll rarely get bored. That is what is great about this field. There's so much opportunity here.

If you get bored with one specialization, develop yourself in another specialized area, and eventually become proficient in two specialized areas. Let's say you get bored with the coding part of software development. But you like the planning work that goes into development. You might consider a move into project management, which is a sorely needed skillset in today's IT organizations. If you become skilled and/or certified in project management, you could lead software development projects more effectively thanks to your coding experience.

So the key to enjoying your work in information technology is to keep learning. Pay attention to boredom since it's telling you when you should look at new things to learn. Also, seek feedback frequently from peers and managers on where your unique strengths seem to show up at work. With people you know well and trust, ask them, too, where you have opportunities to develop and improve yourself at work. A key to advancing in this field is self-awareness. However it's also key to both seek out and constructively use feedback from others on how you're doing in your job and your relationships at work.

I started in this field 20 years ago with no technical degree. Over the years I've moved through a number of different organizations and developed new skills, specializations, acquired a certification and a couple of degrees. After many years of doing strictly technical work, I recently got promoted into the management and planning group for IT.

Now I create science-backed solutions that make our 250-person IT unit at the university more effective on the whole. I help our managers and HR to hire the best information technology professionals. I design ways to train our managers and leaders to excel in their roles. It's been a good run. My success came about from a combination of investing in my education and training, and putting in effort at work to keep improving myself. You can succeed in your own way if you summon the drive and the determination to do it. It all boils down to your personal resolve.

In closing, let me wish you the best of luck. Here's to your successful career in the information technology field!

ABOUT THE AUTHOR

Gale Stafford is an information technology and human resources consultant. He works for the University of Illinois in process improvement, and lives in Urbana, IL with his wife, their two daughters, and a very funny dog.

Gale holds a Masters degree in Industrial-Organizational Psychology from the Chicago School of Professional Psychology.

For more information including free articles on information technology, performance at work, or to sign up for his mailing list, visit Gale's website at http://galestafford.com

You can also connect with Gale on Facebook at http://facebook.com/geektoguru

24331384R00045

Made in the USA
Middletown, DE
21 September 2015